Not Afraid of the Dark:
Thirty Stories of Encouragement, Inspiration, and Perseverance

Darrell W. Reeves, Ed.D

Not Afraid of the Dark

Not Afraid of the Dark

THIRTY STORIES OF ENCOURAGEMENT, INSPIRATION, & PERSEVERANCE

TABLE OF CONTENTS

Forward

Introduction

Part One: Humble Beginnings
There Are No Tigers

Part Two: Prairie Home Companion
The Fascinating Thing About Fascinating Things

Part Three: The Beginning of the End
Same Old Story

Part Four: To There and Back Again
A King's Wonky Plan

Afterward

Not Afraid of the Dark

Not Afraid of the Dark

FORWARD

Encouragement: /inˈkərijmənt,enˈkərijmənt/ Noun. The action of giving someone support, confidence, or hope. "Thank you for all your support and encouragement."

Inspiration: /ˌinspəˈrāSH(ə)n/ Noun. The process of being mentally stimulated to do or feel something, especially to do something creative. "Helen had one of her flashes of inspiration."

Perseverance: /ˌpərsəˈvirəns/ Noun. Persistence in doing something despite difficulty or delay in achieving success. "His perseverance with the technique illustrates his single-mindedness."

Fear: /'fir/ Noun. An unpleasant emotion caused by the belief that someone or something is dangerous, likely to cause pain or a threat. "He is prey to irrational fears."

I grew up as a single child of two parents – Dad worked and my mother stayed home. During my preteen and early teenage years, my parents and I lived in what my father described as a shotgun house. It was commonplace and affordable housing for the era. There were four large rooms in a row off a long, central hallway. At either end of the hallway were the front and back doors. A living room was located at the front of the home. A kitchen and dining area, a bedroom, and finally, a back bedroom and bathroom rounded out the house, save one restroom. The bedroom near the front of the house was mine.

Like many young children, I was afraid of the dark, and at night our house became an extraordinarily dark place. To help cope with my anxiety over the encroaching darkness that came night after night, my mother placed a night light in my room. While it seemed like a good idea to us both, a little illumination to fend off the unknown ghouls, the light only managed to provide more frightening shadows for my imagination than actual comfort. Along the way to restless nights of worry and stress, something changed. After several years of the same horrible night-time pattern, I reached a bubbling point of frustration that caused me to make a decision that would change my life forever; I was going to do something about the dark. I was going to confront it head-on. I would not allow the dark to scare me anymore. You may think I was a brave little engine – and I was to some degree – but I made this bold move out of necessity, not courage. It was too unbearable otherwise.

The back bedroom was the darkest place in our home. It terrified me for years. One night, circling the age of ten, I forced myself to sit in a dark void that was that back bedroom. My mind ran rampant with concoctions. Groping hands were inches away from my skin, sinister eyes, little evil creatures, and any number of demons all awaited my young mind. Even though I was almost scared blind by what could be there with me while the dark pressed in, I told myself nothing was going to harm me and all would be fine. Over and over, I internally repeated my new mantra. I would defeat the dark if it was the last thing I lived to do. I figured it was a fifty-fifty proposition.

Seconds turned into minutes, and minutes turned into an

hour. An hour turned into several hours. My fear began to subside as I learned to embrace my dark surroundings. I sat alone in the dark, in that back bedroom most of the night as my parents slept. They were oblivious to the psychological battle that was taking place in the same home. I then began to understand what was happening to me. There were no monsters, no creatures to grab me and pull me into their lair. It was simply time passing without light. Nothing more. Nothing less.

Over time my fear diminished even more, and I would repeat my time in the darkroom as a mental exercise when necessary. I never did tell my parents about what happened. That night I did it for myself – not anyone else. As a child, I simply felt I would no longer allow darkness to consume me in fear.

INTRODUCTION

Six years into retirement I told myself writing short stories about my life experiences might be a waste of my time. My ideas of authorship were a fledgling notion I truncated with self-doubt and incredulity. Then one day, I began seeing my ideas differently. Why not try to see where these ruminations could take me? As I sat pensively at my laptop one afternoon, I bundled my thoughts together, and in what felt like a herculean effort, I tried to type my history and life experiences into meaningful sentences of insight. At first, my writing felt stilted, difficult, and awkward. Why wouldn't it? I was unpracticed and my skill level was low. After repeated attempts, though, the task becomes easier. The words began to flow more easily and turned into paragraphs that made sense. The maturation process, while still in its nascent stages, was progressing into something more fruitful, more deliberate.

I had so many stories tossing about inside my head. I was compelled to place them on paper. Stories I believe worth reading and discussing. The stories, and writing in general, ultimately were therapeutic for me. With each new story I wrote, my mind could tumble its way through a myriad of emotions, considerations, and outcomes. Each time I'd sit to type I sensed my soul was being fed. I'd like to say that I ultimately came to a grand conclusion after each chapter I wrote. But that wouldn't be the truth. Many times, as I wrapped up a chapter, I intentionally toiled and labored as I thought through what the experience meant, and to a greater extent, how the life example could be viewed through perspectives of encouragement, inspiration, and perseverance. While the validity of my expectations (to encourage, inspire, and perhaps provide some perseverance to those in need) is up to the reader, I believe this endeavor was a gift from God when I needed it most. My Lord and Savior clearly decided I needed something to enhance my life. This was the key that answered two big questions for me.

Why not me? Why not now?

With no siblings and both parents deceased, there is no one else to help recall or tell my stories. But at 65 years old, I feel it's the right time and am comfortable writing them. My experiences, struggles, triumphs, failures, and successes – personal or professional – may not be that different from other people, but there is a reason for that. We all encounter and sometimes struggle with the same challenges life brings our way. I encourage others to write their own stories. They are likely more interesting than someone might have thought.

I share a tale about my youth to begin this book because it speaks to the entanglement that perseverance, inspiration, and encouragement have with fear or our perception of fear. An acronym for fear spells out an antithetical for being afraid of the dark: False Evidence Appearing Real. There is some practicality to the acronym – we are often so afraid we lose sight of reality and get stuck worrying about things that may or may not be true – our latch onto fear is often irrational and can consume us. However, the hedge against full domination by fear seems to be more complex than the acronym allows. You see, there are actual things in life that not only go bump in the night but can hurt you. In fact, the evidence may appear real AND be real simultaneously. How are we to overcome them? By understanding the real dangers of life, how to avoid them in a balanced manner, and not only cope with challenges that befall us but also embrace and overcome them, we are able to trudge through life and perhaps even enjoy it regularly. The unknown and fear of it dissipates. Yes, that is a big statement. By no means have I fully done so. But like the little boy in my story, I can either be afraid of what's in the dark, mitigate some of the dark with some illumination, or work to overcome and embrace my fears.

My journey isn't complete. But I am driven to finish unafraid. It's a choice we all make for ourselves. It's not easy. I chose every day to not give up, to understand my fears, not succumb to them. My lifetime drive, determination, and constant thirst for knowledge are God's gifts, they kept me going. They motivate me to this day. If any reader learns from or is encouraged by these stories this was a worthwhile endeavor.

I dedicate this to my parents, Forest Alden & Virginia Ellen Cottrell Reeves. To my grandfather, Carlyle Cortland

Reeves, a published author. To my wife, Erica Froehlich Reeves, and my three adult children: Rebecca Deanna, Daniel Alden, and Aaron Benjamin Reeves. Also, to my daughter-in-law, Tiffany. My sincere thanks to several encouraging teachers and mentors who inspired me and helped me to see what I could not see in myself. Appreciation and thanks to good friends who accept me for who I am and what I am. I could not have started, organized, and completed this project without my friend, writing teacher, writing collaborator, editor, and marketing consultant, Martin Perez. Finally, I dedicate this writing, effort, and any results from it to my personal Lord and Savior, Jesus Christ. I pray that the book glorifies all that He is and all He has done for my life and my loved ones.

PART ONE: HUMBLE BEGINNINGS

THERE ARE NO TIGERS

While a man walks through a restaurant where he spies a tattoo on an older woman's thin shoulder as she passes him. It's a tiger.

"What a curious tattoo you have," the man remarks. "It's gorgeous."

"The tattoo is from my homeland, Poland," The woman counters and she stops, briefly.

"Oh, is it," the man asks.

The woman continues: "Before I was born, my parents lived in my country's woodlands. They had to build strongholds to live in and used great care when walking in the woods. There were wild animals that stalked the woods – tigers and bears could attack at a moment's notice. Death seemed around every corner. In fact, many people did die from animal attacks."

The man has a questioning look.

The woman finished: "You see, today we stress about so much in life. We fear so much. But ultimately when we walk to the store or a restaurant, what dangers are there? We have things so much better now, even though we are anxious about so much. We lose sight of how good we have things. The tattoo is to remind me I should not stress about the small things or things that ultimately do not matter. There are no bears that might attack anymore. There are no tigers."

Not Afraid of the Dark

CHAPTER 1

THE SALMON KING

In 1972, a small aircraft went missing from Alaska's skyline. While it was something of a story back in the early seventies, the disappearance of the charter plane didn't reverberate across the world, nor did it register as more than inconsequential to the other matters of the world at the time – which was filled with free love, political and social unrest, and a stretching that America felt as it broke from the cocoon of the fifties and sixties "bebop" and sock hop era. Amongst even more noteworthy news items in the hearts and minds of people were the atrocious murders dealt by terrorists during the seventies Olympics in Munich. Concern and awareness were heightened taut like a wire wound on both ends of two stretched hands, and the tension would later lead to boycotts by the United States. This would radically change the way security for athletes and games were managed but also provided something deeper. The psychology of America shifted from safe to tenuous at best. It was the Cold War but at home. The political climate would endure decades of damage from the collapse that would happen during this time. The biggest and brightest political minds would be seen as hopeful drunks falling along an uneven sidewalk. Beyond that jumble of mind-filling, attention-grabbing morose, a different aircraft would grab the big headlines. Twenty-two survivors of a soccer team would crash in the snowy Alps and resort to cannibalism to save themselves and their other living teammates. Movies would purport to show the endurance and subsequent trauma the survivors overcame to reach home in a ridiculous attempt to display the pain and complete depravity the survivors had to overcome to make such a troubling and life-altering decision to eat the person sitting next to them in a flight. History is filled with dead people whose names we forget. Sadly, the lives of those who died would slowly disappear into history books like the names of the deceased so often do. In other areas of life, while this pales in comparison to the astronomical numbers today, the Dow Jones closed above 1,000 for the first time in history. Then it seemed like breaking the four-minute mile in economics. Ultimately, there was plenty in the world to be afraid of in 1972 – never mind the fears of recession and exceedingly high gas prices, and an economy that crashed soon after. The social economic and personal consequences of a nation finding itself and not liking what it sees created an environment that regularly pushed aside individual bouts with happiness and the pursuit of the American dream of independent accomplishment and relationships.

While the missing Alaskan charter craft didn't hang so heavy on the hearts of Americans due to the exigent circumstances of the period, it was a precursor to a strange, almost anecdotal – although statistically supported – mystery that surfaced, and to this day hangs around the neck of Alaska like an albatross and resonates in ways that political unrest and even cannibalism cannot.

The wilderness of Alaska brings an allure to it that seems to engulf the imaginations and even, to a more morbid extent, the practicalities of people who want to get lost, go missing, or inadvertently contribute to the sense of unease in one's life. It comes with the anomaly that a staggering number of people go missing in Alaska. More people than you'd expect or imagine – or even care to expect or imagine. One out of every 617 people in Alaska goes missing. More than 2,000 people go missing every year. It is startling to consider that more than sixty thousand people have gone missing in Alaska since 1988. California, in comparison, has 7.6 missing people per 100,000 (Alaska is at 41.8 missing persons per 100,000).

But, for as odd as it is that so many go missing in a beautiful place, practicality does play a large role. Alaska is riddled with glaciers, caves, and lakes, and has a large geographic swath of land that is pure wilderness. Combine that with rural, sparse populations and fierce, inclement weather, and it's imaginable that so many might disappear. Therefore, it would seem, even more unusual that is the thing that draws people to Alaska the most: the frighteningly stunning wilderness.

There is a sense of romance to the missing persons in Alaska when you get down to it. Who wants to go missing in Des Moines, or Hartford Connecticut? Alaska's appeal is grandiose in ways other states and locations cannot. The nature then of people hoping to get lost, or worse, in Alaska does make sense in a very rudimentary, base level. Our human desire is for identity, attention, and caring. If we don't either get attention, or recoil from it for various reasons, then what better statement to make, than to go missing in Alaska? It's childlike reasoning. If my parents don't pay attention, wait until I'm dead and then they will have to. Alas, all too often child-like ambition drives a lot of what we do culturally, personally, and in life-altering decisions.

On the face of it, for as much strange new world allure and morbid profundity, Alaska really is a hunter and fishermen's paradise. And after being stationed at Eielson Air Force Base near Fairbanks for over a year, I learned to appreciate what "The Last Frontier" state can offer to residents and its visitors. Military members often and readily become residents of the states where they are stationed. Alaska is no exception, despite the statistics and craziness of missing persons, as I mentioned earlier. In fact, despite the numbers, residency is extremely attractive because of the picturesque, rural, and gorgeous environment most of the time. Most of the time, the harsh winters and unending sun can be deterrents to living the Vida Loca. Just one more of the small advantages of becoming an Alaskan resident is applying for what is called a dip netting fishing permit. When you have a dip net permit, you are not required to use a rod and reel to catch salmon. It is considered subsistence fishing so the locals can fill their freezers with fish fillets.

After becoming a resident, I wanted to do the same thing. First, I had to learn dip netting. Luckily, I was not alone in my quest. Dip nets were widely available to rent on the base. A friend took me to the Copper River, where we practiced dip netting salmon that swam upstream. Dip fishing nets are about forty-five inches in diameter, attached to a long aluminum pole, and can be unwieldy if a fisher isn't careful because of their size. We tied ropes to secure ourselves to trees along the riverbanks. Tying ourselves allowed us to gain better footing and traction, lest we fall into the rolling river. As the salmon swam upstream in the raging water they often rested in the calmer areas along the sides of the river. This is where we'd net them. And net them we did.

Salmon are not at all happy about it when captured by a net and tend to fight vigorously for their freedom. The little William Wallaces eventually tire out and their exhaustion leads to demise. The entire experience is interesting, dangerous, and satisfying. We ended up filling our coolers with Red, Silver, and King Salmon fish. My buddy taught me how to fillet them as we caught them. After throwing the remaining guts in the river for all other fish to consume, we left with iced-down salmon fillets to freeze, thaw, and cook later.

The Copper River is unique if not dangerous. A six-hour drive from Fairbanks, there are few amenities, and it is hazardous. Each year there seems to be at least one dip netter fatality on the river, often it's more. Dip netting is allowed from June through September, making it the longest-running dipnet fishery in Alaska.

After gaining experience in dip netting, I was confident enough to go after bigger fish. My friend and I chartered a local guide to take us downriver to a small island in the middle of the Copper River. We hoped to bag larger salmon than we could from the banks. We took the gear necessary for an overnight and were able to fish most of the night. After a handful of attempts, we were able to extract a 60-pound king salmon from the river. We took a few photos of our big catch before we filleted the beast, or it would have been just another fishing story no one believes. I sent a photo to my parents in Indiana who asked a local newspaper to publish it. To this day I have the brief but fun article in my home office. The title of the article is "All Hail to The Salmon King."

Ultimately, whether it is dip net fishing, flying, or just passing the days in Alaska, the reticence to call Alaska anything more than a beautiful vacation destination is unrealistic at best and lacks depth. People do go missing every year – from planes, hiking, canoeing, or whatever mischievous goings-on they might encounter. People do perish from something as innocuous as fishing on riverbanks. Even more, souls pass away from commercial fishing. I'm not trying to be glib, but that is the point. Alaska is a beautiful, dangerous place that rewards the brave and the cautious alike with either a life that is charmed for ages or brief, quick, and concludes too quickly. Often, I feel it's a matter of chance as to what a person might endure. Do they become a casualty of the environment or do they live on with wonderful experiences because of it?

I harken to thinking about life in general when I consider my experiences in the beauty of Alaska. Do I live like I'm dip netting every day – on the edge, in danger? The short answer is no. I am more cautious. But the sense of adventure does bring peace to me. It's a challenge to want to do something. It's even more of a challenge to actually engage in an adventure. Dip net fishing or otherwise, finding a path towards living rather than perhaps "disappearing" in life can be a challenge and adventure in itself. That is something I don't often allow myself to sell short on. There is nothing wrong with the innocuous. It's often required to understand the dangers that do exist. When combined with a healthy perspective – life can and does take on more deep meaning. You don't always have to get lost, in other words, to get found.

CHAPTER 1 FURTHER READING
THE STRUGGLE

"Not only that, but we rejoice in our sufferings, knowing that suffering produces endurance, endurance produces character, and character produces hope." – Romans 5:3-4 ESV

I reflect upon my many travels to places like Alaska and Japan, and even to closer locations in the continental USA. Specifically, I wonder if I honor my many experiences of travel with wonderment, joy, and learning – or if I stop short of considering all that was involved, so I can truly understand what I was being taught? Am I taking what I was given to help gain perspective and share with others – or am I selfishly keeping it to myself as just an enjoyment? I think, perhaps, though I struggle to always accomplish the endeavor, the best use of any travel, voyage, or otherwise, is to share the experience and the wisdom as able to encourage and propel others to understand life even one percent better. It is through the giving of ourselves that we can help our fellow man understand himself or herself.

On the note about identity – I find that we can either seek identity through danger, through self-reflection, or some combination of both. But we cannot find it in something without a full and deep reflection of why we seek our identity in the first place. In Alaska or Des Moines.

CHAPTER 2

FORTY DAYS & NIGHTS, AS TOLD BY PHOTOS

Jack Kerouac single-handedly turned travel on the open road into a romantic idea that would grip our collective imaginations as a nation. Along with countless songs, movies, and other books like On the Road, we quickly became mesmerized by exploring the roads of America, discovering different places, eating exotic new foods, and encountering exciting people. There is a problem with Route 66 heaven, however. Travel never really materializes into the romantic voyage we think it will when we plan. Often, it's the antithesis of what we contemplate. We get tired, arrive late, have countless stops in horrible gas stations, using facilities that are frightening, and the food isn't nearly as grand as we conceive in our minds. Not that travel is all desperation and despair. But on the rare occasion a trip does pan out how we intend, the expense is a nice counterbalance to the sharp enjoyment we find. So, at times, to steady our hearts, we color the trip as well as possible after the fact, through pictures, smiles, and memories that grow more attractive the further we are away from the actual trip.

When I arrived in Denver and met my long-time friend at a large gas station near the airport, I knew there might be some discomfort in store for me. I hadn't imagined the heights to which the discomfort might reach. It was cloudy, raining, and cool outside. Different than the smoldering, one-hundred-degree temperatures I left behind in southern Arizona. It was Sunday, May 31, and I missed watching the Indy 500 on TV, as well as Memorial Day celebrations. But I was committed to the journey my friend and I were about to embark upon, so I forwent other things I enjoyed in favor of my upcoming adventures. I had my phone in tow, ready to snap as many pictures of our trip as I could. I enjoyed cataloging any trip – especially the ones that featured places

I'd never seen in person.

My friend was waiting for me when I arrived. His Dodge Ram turbo diesel truck with dual rear tires and a 33-foot fifth-wheel travel trailer vibrated as it waited for me. The truck and attached trailer were so massive it was as though it had a personality all of its own. It waited, growled, and when we ultimately did leave, relented with burden as it started. Once on the open freeway, the beast of a vehicle was at its happiest. My friend asked me to throw my bags into his RV, run into the station to use the restroom, get food and drink, and then "we're hitting the road" for the next forty days on a road trip adventure.

To be precise, my trip really began the year before. During a previous visit to my friend's home in Colorado, I suggested it might be a great idea for us to take a road trip together. We chose a couple of states I had never visited, Wyoming and Montana. We agreed to share expenses and travel the highways and byways. I wasn't sure how the journey would play out. After a few days with my military buddy, whom I ultimately had not spent extensive time with in thirty years prior, I stumbled upon a fretful realization. He and I were now extraordinarily different people. A lot had changed in the intervening years when we serviced together in Alaska and now, as we both circled retired life.

The fact that we were so different in itself isn't unusual or even a terrible thing. Differences and diversity are what I find most fascinating about the people and places I visit. I enjoy meeting new people – and in essence, my long-time friend really was "new people" for me. And perhaps that was the crux of the matter. I wasn't familiar enough with him to understand the implications of more than five weeks in shared quarters, bumpy roads, shared expenses, and torn ideals about what a vacation consisted of. That was the thing about the new people and places I would typically meet on trips. I didn't then bring them with me once I had been introduced to them, for the next forty days. In effect, my friend and I met each other all over again within the span of a couple of days, recognized our differences, then continued to stick next to each other for thirty-eight more days. And that, I can say, unequivocally, is a significant stretch to spend time with someone new. I submit it's too long a time to spend with anyone new or familiar.

Discomfort is an interesting feeling. At times discomfort can drive a person to create change that matters – at other times, the anxiety that the person encounters can push them into a corner, where they cower, unsure of their next step.

Travel can be a difficult experience regardless of whom the traveling companion is. Preferences, desires, locations, and choices as mundane as where to eat and sleep can grow into monstrosities of a decision. The creature comforts we take for granted on the homestead are tossed aside in favor of a set of unknowns. Agreement or disagreement becomes paramount to success or enjoyment.

Take into consideration that this trip for me would last 40 days and even the smallest decisions exhausted both our capacity for reason on numerous days. However, the entire trip wasn't a loss. We had several enjoyable moments of discussion on several topics ranging from religion and marriage to sports and politics. But in the same way, we were open to talking about so many different topics, we also disagreed on a few things that didn't seem evident from the previous year when the trip manifested. Without fail, the tight quarters seem to engender and exacerbate the potential for disagreement to rear its sometimes-ugly face.

One night – after waking from my bed – I found the floor of the RV rapidly approaching my face as I stumbled in the snug quarters. I would injure my knee and limp for a few weeks after. While not the most critical accident to happen, this incident did hinder my mobility at a time when I needed it most. Slowly, my knee felt better each passing week. But the light pain was somewhat of a constant underlying theme of the trip. Although it would have been easy to just fly home and leave a somewhat uncomfortable situation behind me, I didn't give up. The trip, my friend, and the adventure we encountered might prove to be more challenging than expected, but I still saw value in the time we spent on the road. Considering I was the one who originally suggested the trip, I remained committed no matter what – and likely, to a fault.

As I think about this past trip, I prefer to think about all the wonderful things we saw and did, and what I was able to take pictures of. We visited three national parks: The Grand Tetons, Yellowstone, and Glacier National Park. On their own, the park visits were each worth the time commitment. We went kayaking, whitewater rafting with my wife, hiking, and shared our life stories throughout the long days and into the night on the road. It turned out to be an excellent opportunity to take photos of beautiful country and wildlife, big and small. Since my wife was also separately traveling to northwestern Montana with family, I spent time with her once we arrived in that state, and my friend managed a few days to himself.

One of the best facets of the trip was that we were able to take separate drives, daytime, and evening on the Going to the Sun Road in Glacier National Park. The road is only open for driving two or three months each year due to extreme weather. Ice and snow often prohibit driving near the Canadian border in Glacier. Since I am a much bigger person than my friend (larger in stature and girth), the trip itself was more difficult for me most of the time. I made an earnest attempt every day, but I had difficulty sleeping on the bed I was provided. I was tired much of the trip. Even with these obstacles, including to my health, I survived and even thrived at times. On July 10th, I flew from Bozeman, Montana home to Arizona. All things considered, this was a wonderful trip with a good friend. In the same breath I confidently, and in good conscience, can say I simply don't see taking another trip like it.

I don't condemn the trip, the decision, or even the experiences – including the bum knee – but I am smart at some things. Reflection, learning, and subsequent decision-making are one of those things. So, if I were to take a glibber approach on the trip, I would suggest that the one thing I learned on the adventure was that I didn't want that type of adventure on a repeated basis. I'd done it a little differently.

People come in many shapes and sizes. People also have different character traits that tend to reveal themselves under duress. Travel can be one of the stress points that unexpectedly reveals our true character. Must be why I often feel more tired after a vacation than before. Vacations for rest and relaxation seem great in concept, but rarely great in execution. A lot of hard work goes into planning a trip that is remarkable in destination and experience. Take enough snapshots though, and anything can be remembered fondly, especially as I alluded to before, the distance grows between the trip and reflection.

Emotion recollected in tranquility truly is more substantive if the remembrance is couched in reality, not only what we want it to be. In similar regard, the jaded perspective that only wallows in negative observation is no better than a fantastical creation based on false memories. And so, I do take plenty of photos on trips, vacations, or otherwise. And I wonder, is it to have some fond remembrance when there might not be anything otherwise? Or, as I would be more inclined to hope, I do so because experience can't only be from a subjective experience – truth exists outside of what happens. Only through photos can we gather a better notion of what was out there – not just the romantic ideal - uncolored, unaffected.

CHAPTER 2 FUTHER READING
THE PLANS OF MEN

"Many are the plans in the mind of a man, but it is the purpose of the LORD that will stand." - Proverbs 19:21 ESV

I am chief among planners – my wife is my cohort. She and I plan every trip meticulously. When things don't go according to plan, the discomfort that arises can sideline the good times. Why is that though? The reason is simple. Because of our unfortunate nature, we desire to control what we can and even that which we cannot. Failure is a category filled with plans that went awry. The struggles and challenges found in any trip can be reduced to one remedial thing – *we have determined it was so*. Instead of looking at things as failure though, the alternative is to understand that no matter what happens, if we are guided by the right motivations and spirit, we can rejoice regardless of the perfect picture, the wonderful trip, or the successful number of stops we make.

CHAPTER 3

OF SEASONS, BIKES, AND CORNFIELDS

I grew up in a small southern Indiana city until I was fifteen. We had four decisive seasons each year. The autumns would give countless hours of fun. My friends and I would gather, then pile up leaves, and jump into the surprisingly full, leafy hills that shed from our neighborhood trees. We would later burn the piles, cautiously watching, lest we torch our front and back yards. While I never saw a home burn down due to negligent leaf burning or ash disposal, I am almost certain stories floated around about a local business, a house of otherwise that was raised by carelessness.

The summertime consisted of heat and humidity that would leave us a sticky, sweaty mess with ever-clinging clothes and never-drying bodies. As a chubby child, the specter of clingy clothing made for more discomfort than sweat ever could. Vanity, or the lack thereof, was relentless in its pursuit of dissatisfaction from an awkward, pre-teen body. A cold shower might give a few minutes of relief, but not for long, and not much relief. That said, nothing would spoil our fun.

We were a movie, a postcard, a vignette of small-town Americana in the 60s and 70s, with flags, short haircuts, and ice cream. Wearing striped shirts and jeans, we rode our bicycles like a gang of hoodlums with cards that fluttered rapidly between the spokes of our tires to make "muffler sounds". We chewed gum tirelessly. We snaked down neighborhood streets, driveways and school grounds, storefronts, and "private property" without regard for time or people. We were young and free to spend hour upon hour getting sore legs and an even more sore derriere. I estimate we traversed boundaries that bordered busier streets that I was not to cross for "safety reasons" and because my parents "said so". It was independence feigning as rebellion, in as clean-cut a way possible. But it was still independence, no matter how small the increment.

We played baseball and football on a large vacant lot which was later owned by an auto dealership – simply so they could park their unsold newer vehicles. This momentary lapse in kid-friendly logic destroyed our fun until we found another area to play our games. I remember my mother calling out from our front porch down the street. It was time for me to come home for dinner on the regular. It was the only thing that brought me in. Otherwise, we were the Lords of Flatbush, reimagined as pre-teen boys, minus the sultry eyes, cowlicks, and fighting.

I would bundle up with a heavy coat, stocking hat, neck scarf, and gloves during the winters for the daily long walks to my elementary school, and later to my junior high. There was no drop-off or pick-up from my parents. Dad needed our only car, dilapidated as it was, to get to work. My mother did not drive. If there was snow and ice (there always was snow and ice during winters) I wore rubber snow boots up to my calves. When the chilling wind hit my face, it felt like it was going to shear my face clean off with shards of glass. Of course, that never happened, but that did not make my face feel any better, even in retrospect. To this day, Southern

Indiana and the Midwest can manifest some harsh winter storms that allow the neighborhood kids to build snow forts and snowmen. The snowball fights we had as kids are a good memory.

We heated our four-room, shotgun-style home with coal that burned in a large furnace in our basement, below our house. While the coal was warming, it was a spectacularly messy and inefficient way to keep warm. When my father and I would drive to the nearby coal yard to purchase chunks of mined coal, because we had no pickup truck, Dad would place an old quilt or blanket in the trunk of the car and fill it as much as he could. With the extra weight, the rear of the car almost touched the road. We would later unload and lug the coal bucket-by-bucket to a cellar near our aging furnace. Coal dust and black soot are dirty and not beneficial to inhale but we had plenty of both. Many coal miners would eventually suffer and die from the notorious "black lung" affliction; this was not lost on me as we trudged from the car to the house and back again, and again.

Springtime always felt like it brought an opportunity for annual rebirth and warmer outside temperatures. We rode our bikes to school and would play outside without the cumbersome outer clothing that winter required. There was a nearby field where wildflowers would grow. I would pick a few wildflowers to take to my mom. She always acted like she loved to receive them but I estimate she did not really want weeds in her clean house. In the middle of my freshmen year, my father decided to sell our home in a great city neighborhood and the nostalgia of childhood abruptly halted. The thought of seasons and reminiscing was cut with a harsh reality that I would lose all my friends, all my cool spots to hang out, and all the identity that I grew up knowing.

We moved twenty miles away to a smaller town, a rural agricultural area. The move was devastating emotionally. I had to leave all my childhood friends and experiences behind for a countryside filled with corn, soybean, and wheat fields. I was forced into a much different life, from city to country kid. It did not go at all well for me. I was suddenly riding a school bus with mean country farm kids who made fun of the new kids – namely, me. As time passed, I, of course, learned to embrace my new surroundings and things improved slightly. I attended the balance of my freshmen, sophomore, junior, and senior years at a small country high school that graduated seventy-three students in May 1976.

I like to say that the move to the country, though unprovoked, unexplained, and impractical, was good for the family in retrospect. But the benefits that blossomed from the abrupt move were long and slow in coming – years even – and may have nothing to do with the actual move itself but were simply the outcome of the natural course of life. It was like getting nudged into the river from a canoe by my father. Only downstream, the rapids break with whitewater and turbulence tossing about. I eventually made my way back to land and even walked again, but it didn't really have to do with that initial nudge. I say without a doubt my life changed significantly. Likely, it didn't have to. Dad never told me or my mother why. He died, never having explained the practicality of uprooting his family.

Dad's drive to work ended up being longer as he didn't change jobs, and the school I attended during part of my day and later got a custodial job at, was filled with a few country bullies, and kids I didn't know. At fifteen years of age, I was either at the prime of my life ready to turn into a young man with direction, looks, and appeal, or I was going to be reduced to emotional rubble because of insecurities and doubts any teen might have. When dad shuttled us away from every friend I knew since grade school, he in effect canceled my childhood and forced me to grow up faster than I wanted, or ever expected. There would be no more Americana, no more bike riding freely and casually with friends. I would have to focus and work on a whole new group of friends – knowing full well that in a couple short years, I'd again have to leave for college or a job away from home.

As the saying goes, we can never return home again – not to the way it was. And my early childhood and teen years were gone forever because of an impetuous and strange decision by my father. It was then that the allure of something new struck me solidly. I balanced a building inward sense of guilt for a couple of years after the move. I didn't want to leave my mom and dad alone, as mom's health was always failing, and back then dad wasn't exactly the caring, attentive sort. But I could feel my sense of displeasure and desire for travel, adventure and growth beyond the country grow more every day. I did get to move out and away – but not without reticence for leaving mom, and an understanding that home wasn't home anymore. How could it be – I was drawn away.

CHAPTER 3 FURTHER READING
THE DARKNESS AND THE LIGHT

"The light shines in the darkness, and the darkness has not overcome it." – John 1:5 ESV

As I grew up and encountered what I would consider traumatizing moves, marriages, and more, I found comfort that even in the darkest times I could relent. I don't do so under my own power – like I did when I was a boy in the dark. But I've come to understand that no light can be overtaken by darkness, in life experience, spiritual existence, or physical location. The fact is we may not always know why things happen – and feel the darkness pressing upon us. When we understand the winning equation, we can't help but feel like we've chosen the winning team. Yes, trauma is real. Yes, darkness can invade a man's life. But, when we remember the truth, that light shines no matter how heavy the darkness may seem, we can move towards the light with hope and joy despite all circumstances.

CHAPTER 4

LIFE AFTER MY PARENTS –

A TASTE OF FREEDOM

The country was fine. The rural, agricultural make-up of cornfields and grass, two-lane roads, and crows lend to a serene charm that is both isolating and quaint. Make no mistake, the lack of people is something of an acquired taste. Especially, if a child has grown up around a city life that provided friends, adventure, and variety at a moment's notice. In a city, it's easy to get lost in something new. In a rural community, you find yourself alone. A lot. And, if a person is alone, a lot, a sense of suffocation quickly overcomes the loneliness that's sure to follow. Like rats trapped in a maze, the sense of urgency, then, to escape becomes paramount.

Mixed emotions ruled the morning I left to start college. My mother was tearful and sad. She was vacant, the prospect of her baby boy leaving home for good enveloped her mind. Her only child was leaving the nest and she would miss me terribly – she would miss our conversations, our sharing, and our private insights with each other. We had always been close, my mother and I, and we often would talk for great lengths of time. She treated me as a peer. I was a confidant and a shoulder to cry on. As I matured, I felt like my mother even grew dependent on my relationship since my father was absent most of the day.

My parents had a volatile relationship and that often led to parental arguments. My odd, sometimes tenuous position, as a child arbiter was not inconsequential. Most of the time my father did not discuss his relationship issues with either me or my mother and as a result, I eventually acted as a marriage counselor to my mother. These circumstances while not normal, were also not as uncommon as I might expect in families. Overall, though, the negative influence of having to be the rudder that steadied the ship in my young life left me with profound consequences that would later manifest themselves in my own marriages, my parenting style, and even my work career. I did cry goodbye tears on this day, but I also had feelings of joy. I was ready to try to blossom into something other than the solution to my parents' inadequate communication skills.

For the first time in my life, I knew what freedom could be when I left home. The 75-mile drive to my first semester in college was my declaration of independence – a stamp on my world experience that said a new Darrell was in town. It was time to rebrand myself and reveal who I truly was – or at least, wanted to be. I knew my mother and my relationship would suffer because of the reliance she had on our cabal. And it also saddened me because I felt needed by her. But my travels also meant that I could relinquish my role as an all-too-young counselor and enjoy my youth. Now I could focus on myself. And thus, the mixed emotions were at their height. Should I feel guilty for leaving my mother behind in her struggles? Should I be okay with "starting my new life?"

When I arrived on campus, I was assigned a bottom-floor room within an older, all-male dormitory. Soon thereafter, I met my new roommate. Both of us would have preferred to have lived alone but this was not going to happen as a first-year student. I brought my stereo radio and turntable and all my vinyl albums. My roommate took advantage of my collection and would often play them without my permission. It was not strange for me to return after a night out and find records playing, and him not even present.

As an only child, it was my first time understanding that my stuff was not always respected as "my stuff." One time I came home after a day of classes and found wooden bunk beds in the room. I had the bottom bunk. My roommate had not consulted me about this decision. He had done it and that was that. I was not at all pleased and I went to my residence assistant or RA to ask for another roommate. The request was of course denied. Final room assignments had been made.

Every college campus, especially during the free for all seventies, had its share of alcohol and illicit drug use. My college was in the state of Indiana where you had to be at least age 21 to consume alcohol. But a quick drive over a river bridge took you to Illinois, where the legal drinking age was only eighteen. To wit, to a student, we took advantage of the discrepancy in legal age and distance. Some took more advantage than others, but most took advantage. My roommate, for example, spent more time partying than in class. He was in the same degree program as I was and he did not even return his second year. I would never see or hear from him again. I wonder from time to time whatever happened to him: likely off somewhere playing someone else's records, while smoking, drinking beer, and sleeping on bunk beds.

During my second year in the college dormitory, I was introduced to a much better situation. My assigned floor was on the upper floors, and I got a new roommate, of course. The new roommate drove home every weekend for various reasons, so I had the room to myself. I didn't care if my new roommate went home to be with his parents, off to some foreign destination to enjoy a relaxing time, or disappeared so he could deal in nefarious trades of some sort. All I knew was that it was wonderfully quiet, peaceful, and mostly just mine. The solitude was appreciated, and allowed me the time to think about my life, what I wanted to do, and how I would go about doing it. I was a bit of a planner even then. It worked (and still does) as plans give me the opportunity to preemptively develop contingencies when needed, and agility as appropriate. It was a perspective on life that my upcoming military experience would support greatly.

The allure of freedom, the idealistic painting I created in my mind was both captivating and a mirage for me. The main reason is that I found while I had a mind big enough to see the future and the latitude given to me, my heart was not able to digest the volume of responsibility I took on. That's not to say I was an abject failure by any stretch. I found a modicum of success in almost every avenue I approached. But I also encountered significant failure I struggle to comprehend fully to this day. College and roommates were the least of the challenges I would face – but in hindsight, they set the groundwork and tone, and revealed a path of ever-increasing difficulty I would see as I explored the world and the people in it. Some of my biggest challenges were also where I see the most success, however. In my career and my relationships, the precarious relationship between success and failure would become something I learned how to balance, overcome, and grasp more fully. I was able to learn and flourish. It was not easy. It is not easy. But I progress.

CHAPTER 4 FURTHER READING
TRAIN UP A CHILD

"Train up a child in the way he should go; even when he is old he will not depart from it." - Proverbs 22:6 ESV

"Fathers do not provoke your children to anger, but bring them up in the discipline and instruction of the Lord." - Ephesians 6:4 ESV

At times, the truth is easy to believe – but hard to apply in my everyday life. Like anyone, I enjoy sharing wisdom with others, but at the same time, struggle to manifest the truth in my own life in practical ways. In particular, the verse about children spins me in circles. I know that if I concentrate on teaching my children – even as an adult now – in the proper ways to follow truth, the wisdom will not be lost. And I know through the lack of training my parents provided I experienced some struggles of oppression. I know I can change my habits. So, I point to the truth for anyone who will see it: pour into your children truth, perspective, and wisdom, and it will benefit them much more than any trinket you can buy them at Christmas – more than any clothing, shoes, toys, or other items. It is not the things my parents bought me that I remember – it is the words they said or didn't say. It is the time and the heart of who they were that I recall most. It is the training I received that I use for my own life and I pour into my children.

CHAPTER 5

THE DRIVE TO MY FIRST WEDDING LEFT ME

WITH CONCERNS

The drive to church for my first marriage riddled me with
more than a few concerns. I should have listened to my
rational self-talk more than my poor, smitten lustful heart.
How well did I really know my fiancé? How well did I really
know her parents or her extended family? How well did I
know the entirety of the situation? The clear answer is that I
didn't know my fiancé well at all. I didn't have any
understanding of her extended family or their shady pasts. I
had no clue the power her parents held over her.

Forty-four years after the fact and it is easier to question my thought process at the time. I would pay an emotional, mental, physical, and financial toll for my decision to get married. It is a poetic justice to my haphazard, yet exhausting approach to nuptials. While I would not learn very much from the experience back then, I have pristine clarity now on many things.

It was during my first two years at college that I met my first wife. She lived on a farm in the local area. I eventually would meet her family. They were so welcoming at first. Little did I know years later how this would change. Nice and welcoming later turned into nasty and suffocating. They went to war against me. Freedom, as it turned out, came at an unexpected price – the cost was my mental stability, gaslighting, and threatening behavior to my perspectives on how the world worked.

After we married, my new bride and I eventually moved to the same town where I had first attended college. She and her family all lived nearby in a rural agricultural area, or as I often referred to it: "farm country." I decided to work in retail sales for a while, then had a few temporary jobs after that, before slaving as a shipping and receiving clerk at a local electrical supply company. During my time at the electrical company, I gained a strong command of warehouse management, understood, and practiced how to drive a forklift, and learned how to make "over the road" deliveries to industrial and commercial construction sites. After a few years of working at low pay for a boss who did not appreciate hard work, in a town I knew I would not ever provide much of a future, I decided to visit a military recruiter and put George Bailey behind me. I was not going to be stuck in the small town. I would make something better for myself and my wife. I had been forced to move to a small town before in my life – I wasn't about to settle again. Not when I had the wherewithal to do otherwise.

To put it succinctly, my first father-in-law was not a nice man. Shortly after marriage, he bought my wife and me some bedroom furniture, which he claimed was a gift. As the months went on, I could see how he was going to use this gift to try and leverage control in our marriage. As my sense of his underlying motivations grew, I decided to pay him in full for the furniture. I wanted to remove any doubts about who lived my wife's and my life. We cleaved to each other, not our parents for direction or control in our own lives. This was not well received. While I was not surprised, I was clear in my statement; I would not be manipulated, monetarily or otherwise.

When I joined the military and was eventually assigned overseas, my father-in-law was not happy. His only daughter had been taken away from their homeland. To me, it was obvious that he struggled with abusive mental health issues. I did not want to be anywhere near the behavior. Moving away seemed like the best answer for us.

My wife was fine with the decisions we made to start living our lives in the world, away from close family. We stayed for a spell in Japan, which proved a fantastically unique experience. After my three-year tour ended in Japan, I was assigned to a base in the desert southwest of Arizona. After almost three years at my second base, though, my wife was ready for a child. We had waited because we were not sure if we wanted a family at first.

During the pregnancy, my wife began to exhibit mental health issues of her own, and they began to manifest themselves in a variety of ways. I tried not to correlate her newfound behavior with her father's but it was difficult to separate the two. By the time we had our baby, she was acting in a manner I had never seen before. It was complex, not clear-cut, or simple. There were shades of a struggle at first and I wasn't sure what to make of it. She decided she wanted to move back to the Midwest near her family and I did not want to return. I think a confluence of forces that included mental health, my work, and her struggles in early motherhood eventually led us down the path of divorce.

After the brutal divorce, I was absolutely devastated. I was alone, without my daughter, and ordered to pay my now ex-wife support for a child that I would not see for another twenty years. What was ahead of me was a divisive and gut-wrenching journey to find something or someone to take away the tremendous pain I felt.

CHAPTER 5 FURTHER READING
WARNINGS

"Son of man, I have made you a watchman for the house of Israel. Whenever you hear a word from my mouth, you shall give them warning from me. If I say to the wicked, 'You shall surely die,' and you give him no warning, nor speak to warn the wicked from his wicked way, in order to save his life, that wicked person shall die for his iniquity, but his blood I will require at your hand. But if you warn the wicked, and he does not turn from his wickedness, or from his wicked way, he shall die for his iniquity, but you will have delivered your soul." - Ezekiel 3:17-19 ESV

The fact of the matter is that we often see warnings in our lives and ignore them because we want to do what we want to do. Despite the red flags we encounter, we set them aside until we sufficiently explore the path we've decided. Yet, when all is said and done, we mourn and gnash teeth because of the difficulties that have befallen us. How is it that we think we want to control a situation, then decry the outcome as though we play no role in determining the outcome?

I think that playing the victim is tantamount to using excuses after the fact. If we play with fire, we must accept the consequences to the burning. The world has consequences for our ill-suited intentions, no matter how well-intentioned we are. So, in order to find the best outcomes, we must keep our ear to the ground, so to speak. Watch for warnings and heed them. Pain is not to be trifled with. Emotional damage is not something easily dismissed. We need to be cautious and act like it.

CHAPTER 6

NEW BEGINNINGS, OR…HOW DID I END UP ON THE OTHER SIDE OF THE PLANET?

In 1982, I arrived over Memorial Day weekend at one of the largest U.S. military installations in Japan and was perplexed by the current situation: how in the world did I end up on the other side of the planet? Six months earlier, I was living and working in a small southern Indiana town. A few conversations with military recruiters, a favorable aptitude test, and a physical exam later, and I was an official enlisted member of the U.S. Air Force. Suddenly, I was in

San Antonio, Texas with other men enduring eight weeks of basic training. We did our best to make it through rigorous and challenging days. Of course, most of us would graduate and never see each other again.

Soon enough, I was on a bus to Wichita Falls, Texas to attend technical training. My job would be air transportation. A few weeks into tech school, I returned to my dormitory room to find a large package that was shoved under the door into my room. It was a welcome packet from my first military assignment. On the outside of the folder were the words "Welcome to the Gateway to the Far East." I looked at it with amazement and some fear. Yokota Air Base is forty-one kilometers, or about twenty-five miles, from Tokyo, one of the largest cities in the world. If you were to combine the populations of New York City and Los Angeles, they do not add up to the larger size of Tokyo.

The culture shock itself was a lot to take in for a native Indiana Hoosier who had never flown on an airplane until starting my military career. I had to contend with a language I couldn't understand, signs I couldn't read, different landscapes, and vehicles with steering wheels on the right side as they drove on the wrong side of the road.

If I were to put it into a box of words that somewhat

described the cultural differences that made the most impact between America and Japan, I would start with the fact that gesturing can get a man in trouble. Something as simple as a thumb down means "go to hell" in Japan, as opposed to the lighter disapproval it shows here. Even more subtle gesticulations like rubbing the back of my neck implies I had no idea about what's being said. Dress wear is important and can cause significant displeasure if not standard. Formality was key to making any cultural inroads.

I learned that asking questions or making mistakes in Japan leads to larger consequences than we tend to ascribe in the United States. As a result, the decision-making process is much more languid, slow-boiling and tends to make the impatient recognize their faults wildly. Something that really is different though is the lack of true emotion or feeling displayed in the Japanese culture. Expression takes on a different form than in a bold, first nation like ours. While the outcome is a more positive nature ostensibly, the truth of how a Japanese person might feel lay somewhere underneath, quietly burbling away. A critical, and perhaps even alarming and overwhelming cultural shift in my new country was the preference for remaining silent as opposed to being outspoken. Even at my younger age, I had a tendency to be outspoken about the things I was passionate about. One of the most American things we have is a right to share with the world how we feel about any given topic, much less things that really motivate us. In Japan, the shouting on the rooftops about anything is strictly curbed. Silence is golden.

I was fortunate that my assigned organizational squadron provided me with a welcome sponsor. Upon my arrival, however, the sponsor was nowhere to be found. So, I buckled up and did what I could to establish myself. I was twenty-four years old and not exactly helpless or afraid by this point. Adventure was closer to me than ever and I was set to take it on.

The following week, I was called to my new squadron commander's office and asked why I hadn't waited for my sponsor to arrive. I let them know since my base sponsor wasn't there, I wasn't also going to wait for assistance that might not arrive. I received a firm warning about the importance of following orders, and what happens when enlisted men don't. Rules are something I could not side-step or consider alternatives to. Rules were to be followed and that was it. In the military, when rules aren't followed, people can die, it was that simple. While the stern talk wasn't that specific, I was told I was not to break orders again, or I would face severe consequences. It bruised my ego but wasn't without merit, and I eventually accepted the truth of what was being said – not resting on the delivery of the message.

A few months into a three-year tour of duty, I was well on my way. Good things were about to happen in my young life. I worked at a huge military airport. It was nonstop excitement. My wife and I lived in base housing. We made friends with other families. I completed thirty hours of college credit toward a bachelor's degree I would later obtain in 1990. This far-away place turned out to be one of the greatest experiences of my life. One of many provided by my military service.

CHAPTER 6 FUTHER READING
WHAT'S IN STORE

"But, as it is written,

"What no eye has seen, nor ear heard,

nor the heart of man imagined,

what God has prepared for those who love him."

- 1 Corinthians 2:9 ESV

Early in life, I had grown accustomed to doing what I could do for myself. I had to learn early and quickly. I could make my own way. Little did I understand that if I am able to relinquish the reins humbly then the Lord would greatly move me to places and experiences, I could never have guessed I'd be a part of. I grew up in a small town, sheltered by two parents who loved me but were struggling to live their own lives. When I left home, I stuck it out "on my own," full of life and vigor. I would run into a wall of relational and emotional upsets that could sideline the best players in any sport. But as I learned and obeyed the command to let go, and follow instead, I found my life gained so much. I am not perfect, nor will I ever be while alive – But I do know that I strive to allow my desires to submit to those of God, for He has much more in store for me than I could ever hope. I encourage others to do the same. We can continue our imperfect journey together.

CHAPTER 7

FROM EXTREME HEAT

TO EXTRAORDINARY COLD

Temperatures in Arizona can reach upwards of 115 or 120 degrees in the middle of summer, and 50 years ago it was only incrementally less. Figure temps in the 110s plus my military dress, and on a daily basis the pervasive, sweltering heat invaded my lungs and pores, causing me to almost suffocate in the stifling conditions. Heat isn't the only thing in Arizona but it's a decisive factor more frequently than not, in whether people want to move out west. The term "dry heat" casually describes Arizona summers from the uninitiated, as though dry heat is a plausible general descriptor of weather, like "it's raining cats and dogs," or as if the term somehow reduces the severity of the heat to an innocuous level of discomfort. But there is nothing casual about dry heat. It isn't dry like you might imagine dry – perhaps an envelope sheltering people from the brutality of the burning Sun. Instead, dry heat is palpable, like walking through a dryer set on high tumble, only with less movement or air, and more heat. Arizona's air firmly grips your lungs, pulls them downward to your feet, and drains any bit of moister in your body; the heavy heat back then depressed my skin, my mindset, and my general countenance. But after three years of living in the desert southwest, the military moved me to the complete opposite climate at the top of the world.

Fairbanks, Alaska is nestled in the cold interior of the 49th state, and one of the more inhospitable places on earth when it comes to weather. The winters are eight months long, with temperatures at times 40 degrees below zero. If you've not experienced forty below, it's rude in its welcome. When in 40 below temperatures, the body experiences what I call a "pucker". The fingertips and outer extremity's blood vessels constrict tightly. There is an immediate feeling of burning on the fingers and a pain as it creeps up the forearms and legs. Located approximately twenty-five miles from the City of Fairbanks, and eight miles from the small town of "North Pole," Eielson Air Force base would be my third active-duty military assignment in the military. My apartment was in the North Pole.

There was an oddly large Santa Claus house in the North Pole, and it was, as you might guess, a year-round tourist magnet. Family would send me unmailed stamped envelopes so I could mail them back with the North Pole, Alaska 99705 postmark. Depending upon the time of year, the amount of daylight could range from almost twenty fours in peak summer, to less than 60 minutes in the depths of the cold, eight-month-long winter. This darkness had long been proven to impact residents' overall mental state. Depression and alcoholism were common. Alaskan moose, bear, and caribou were among the many wildlife that roamed freely in the vast, almost empty countryside.

Living and working in Alaska was challenging. The brutal, freezing temperatures were similar only to a few other places on the planet. Freezing weather garments were a constant to protect body parts from frostbite, and vehicles were equipped with special devices that assisted in "normal" operation during ten to forty degrees below zero. When I drove the highway to and from the military base, it was not unusual for vehicle exhaust fumes to turn into ice fog. Ice fog made things difficult to see. Methodical, slow driving was the only way to avoid contact with anyone or anything. It was unnerving. Yet, with all the negatives, there were many positive takeaways from living there as well. The aurora borealis or "northern lights" was a colorful feast for the eyes and is truly unlike anything else I had seen. The beauty of the land was mesmerizing at times.

My second wife and I were assigned to Alaska for three years. The military considers it an overseas tour, so families were allowed to live there with military members. However, I spent much of wintertime alone since the eight-month winter cycle in Alaska did not agree with my wife and she traveled back to the lower 48 states. Living and working at my job at a small military passenger and transport cargo terminal filled my days. I made great friends and we shared this unique Alaska experience together. One of my children was born in a military hospital located at the nearby U.S. Army Fort Wainwright because my Air Force base only had a clinic. I look back on this time with absolute amazement.

First, because I managed to survive the experience; second, because I survived the experience.

CHAPTER 7 FUTHER READING
ANXIOUS

"Rejoice in the Lord always; again I will say, rejoice. Let your reasonableness be known to everyone. The Lord is at hand; do not be anxious about anything, but in everything by prayer and supplication with thanksgiving let your requests be made known to God." - Philippians 4:4-7 ESV

Do not be anxious. It's crazy how much we disregard such wisdom in our lives – and at the smallest of events and circumstances. As I consider my life, I am astounded by the number of times I allow myself to feel anxiety and worry, for no reason other than I can't see the outcome. As I trust in God more, I find I am better equipped. While I still encounter anxiousness (and frankly, there are medical explanations for some anxiety, so I do not want to marginalize those struggles) I am more easily persuaded that the Lord would have me rest in His joy, not my troubles.

Something that was shared with me was helpful in reducing stress, elevating awareness of my actions, and a general encouragement: The Holy Spirit is with believers all the time, in everything I do, and in every decision I make. I am never alone. When I make bad decisions, He is with me. When I make good decisions, He is with me. What I do knowing that is now my responsibility.

CHAPTER 8

RETURNING TO MY MIDWESTERN ROOTS

After I left my third military base in Alaska, I requested a base closer to my midwestern roots. My years in Japan, Arizona, and Alaska were an adventure but now I wanted to live near my parents who were now getting on in age. I applied for and was granted a special duty assignment where I would work at Military Airlift Command (MAC) operations at the St. Louis, Missouri International Airport. My parents were going to be a 3-hour drive away. I was lucky to receive this assignment as many applied but only a few were selected.

I felt blessed and proud to be there - I was part of an elite few considered the "best of the best" in their career field.

The cherry on top? I was also nearby the southern Indiana town where I grew up. After ten years of living in three places vastly different from one another, I learned to appreciate my homeland. About once a month, I would leave after my airport evening shifts ended and traveled an interstate highway through the state of Illinois. Not too long thereafter, I was back in Hoosier land. My parents were always pleased to see me for a few days. It was reciprocal. After dad retired from his job as a maintenance manager at a large department store, my father worked for his friend who owned laundromats within nearby small communities. He maintained the clothes washers and dryers and helped with building maintenance and custodial work. My mother was devoted to various hobbies and projects that kept her busy most of the time.

During the nine years I was away, both my parents developed additional health issues. I was glad I was able to spend more time with them while I still could. My parents were also able to spend time with my son who was born back in Alaska. From ages three to four, he loved hanging out with his grandparents. I felt like having my son around them was a gift for my parents. They always shared how fortunate they felt to see their grandson. This was especially valuable as my ex-father-in-law never made it easy for Mom and Dad to visit my first child, their granddaughter.

A final bonus of living closer to home was my own time with relatives I had not seen in ages. But living in the St. Louis area was spectacular for a variety of reasons even beyond the family and friends aspect.

I'd eventually buy my first home near the airport. There was always lots to take in and do around the metro area. I took my father to pro baseball games. His health was still good enough to do active things and he enjoyed them so much.

As the world often prescribes, however, all good things come to an end – that was two years later for me. A new military conflict had arisen in a desert region across the globe from my idyllic return home. The Gulf War and subsequent Desert Storm military operation reared its ugly historic head. A paid separation from active service prompted me to make difficult choices. Should I stay and potentially be forced out of my current position by a congressionally mandated "military drawdown" or accept money and return to civilian life? I decided to separate, sell my home, and move to

Arizona. My parents would sell their home as well and move to Arizona along with me, as they had planned many years prior.

CHAPTER 8 FURTHER READING
UNDERSTANDING

"May we have strength to comprehend with all the saints what is the breadth and length and height and depth, - Ephesians" - 3:18 ESV

I say all good things come to an end. What I mean to say is that all earthly things come to an end. The goodness that emanates from God never ceases. By embracing the goodness that extends beyond our time here we can accept even the endings with joy. It is with this knowledge that we trudge forward, living life with the comfort of knowing our true journey has only just begun.

The difficult part in this ideal vision that God shares with us about eternity is not believing this future exists, but to live like it does. There are so many things that I used to believe were true about the Bible but I never reflected in my everyday life. I think that's a step in the maturation process as a Christian man. As I have moved further along in my faith walk, I have begun to embrace and reveal my belief in how I live, not just in my intellectual understanding.

I would encourage you to do the same with God's promise of a future with Him – where we don't mind things ending because God will start something new. It's something I must relearn every day. Fortunately, God's grace is sufficient for my lack of understanding, and adherence to His word, and His patience is everlasting.

CHAPTER 9

NICE NEAT LITTLE PACKAGES

I slowly leaned back in my office chair and stated, firmly, decisively, but with compassion for my employee's plight: "When you behave like the offenders we supervise that's a serious problem."

My employee sat quietly and said nothing. After reading them their disciplinary reprimand, I asked if they had a response. As the officer signed the document to acknowledge receiving it, their answer was "No."

From 2006 to 2016, I was a unit supervisor and chief of a department. One of the undesirable duties of any management position that supervises employees is responding to and addressing poor job performance in an appropriate manner. My end goal was always to provide guidance so that employee behaviors would improve and make for a better workplace. When I considered that the work as a probation officer is challenging in nature, to begin with, the added pressure of performance reviews and corrective discipline then, seemed insurmountable at times. Yes, the work of an adult or juvenile probation officer could be, at times, extremely difficult – but it didn't excuse us from stewarding the department's staff behavior in the right direction when it fell off. After being a case officer for twelve years, working the streets and rural areas of southern Arizona, I interviewed for and was eventually promoted to a supervisory role. As a result, I was responsible for a group or a unit of eight to twelve officers who supervised criminal offenders. So, in effect, I knowingly had jumped from the frying pan into the fire of possible employee tensions and performance challenges. There was a learning curve.

After taking the job, I quickly encountered things I had not anticipated. As the "boss," I could no longer be their friend or peer. I was now management staff, and that required me to comport myself in a different manner. Not only did I have a job to do, but there was also a layer of decorum that was necessary to lead a team, rather than be content *as a part of a team*. My job was to instruct, make fair and impartial decisions, and model what a good officer and supervisor should be. The added responsibility was for the sole purpose of ensuring the department was aligned with the spirit of the law and its established mission and vision. All of it was for a song of a five percent pay raise, and a lot of extra headaches.

Generally, staff can accomplish their work with minimal complaints if trained properly. As a boss, I discovered an appreciation for staff because they usually require little to no oversight. It was the ten to twenty percent that required the sixty to seventy percent of time that created a mental and emotional drain. The difficult employees kept caring supervisors and administrators awake at night, wrestling with correct decisions, proactive behaviors, and even caused doubt and consternation. Poking the bear among their peers, the time-consuming employee can challenge the rules or push their personal agenda forward to see how far they can go. Having received one reprimand earlier in my career, I understood how it felt to be the recipient of progressive discipline. I learned from my past mistakes.

When I would see disruptive, bullying behavior, it was my job to shut it down immediately and without hesitation. Bullying behavior, unfortunately, was something I became intimately familiar with. If not stopped quickly it was bad for staff morale and the organization's long-term health. I encountered some of the most challenging staff when I was a line supervisor or chief probation officer; those whose work ethic, strangely enough, I admired. With a passion for their job, they sadly would allow themselves to circumvent policy and procedure and take matters into their own hands to accomplish their goals at any cost. These were often the officers I disciplined the most. They were also the ones who took time away from many other obligations.

Prior to providing a reprimand I was once told, "You don't get it. You want us to follow all the rules. But life often doesn't work like that. Solutions do not always come in a nice, neat little package."

Upon reflection, that employee was right. They were also short-sighted though. It's true life doesn't come in nice, neat little packages that contain everything and anything to make things work. But that is the exact reason we need rules and order. Without guidelines, people could decide whatever they want is the best solution or response – certainly, anarchy has never been an effective barometer for progress, productivity, or efficiency. Instead, a lack of order or rules is simply a way for those who can't improve (or don't want to improve) to sidestep accountability. Life is messy – but an effective counter to the disorganization that befalls us in life is to use rules to propel us forward in the mire that is there sometimes. Life was, and isn't, about nice, neat little packages. But it's the nice, neat little packages that serve as reminders of our humanity, goals, and efforts to succeed.

CHAPTER 9 FUTHER READING
SELF-CONTROL

"For this very reason, make every effort to supplement your faith with virtue, and virtue with knowledge, and knowledge with self-control, and self-control with steadfastness, and steadfastness with godliness, and godliness with brotherly affection, and brotherly affection with love." - 2 Peter 1:5-7 ESV

God understands that I live in the world — even as I try to understand that I am sanctified from it (Meaning, that spiritually I am set apart, as a child of God, not from the earth). So, He also understands that my earthly failures — while driven by my own flesh — run counter to His character, but are a necessary part of being alive here, today. It is with that relational grace that He affords me mercy and forgiveness. And it is that mercy, grace, and forgiveness I have to carry with me in any job (volunteer or otherwise) if I'm to exhibit His nature of self-control and steadfastness.

When I look at the time I spent as a Unit Supervisor or

Chief Probation Officer and all the relationships I managed, effectively or not, I try to look at them through the eyes of what our Lord sees. People are flawed and weak when acting outside of God's guidance. I must have compassion. For it is compassion I seek when I act outside God's will myself. It helps me understand people's motivations and lead them better. Even outside of the work positions, whenever I find myself in a leadership role – I do so with the encouragement that God placed me there – and the caution to understand that He placed me there to guide His people, not my own agenda.

CHAPTER 10

MANAGING DYSFUNCTION

I began my search for full-time employment when I returned to Arizona in 1992. Leaving active-duty military service after eleven great years was difficult but I was committed to it. While serving in the military, I gathered classes over an eight-year period and earned my college degree in 1990. Back in civilian life, I wanted to find something that would pay reasonably well with good benefits. Most importantly I wanted a job that would challenge, teach, and inspire me.

When given a recruitment sheet for a Senior Clerk job at

a county adult probation department, I decided to apply. At my interview, I was asked what my long-term goals were. My reply made perfect sense to me. I figured if I worked for adult probation I might as well be an adult probation officer. After the interview, I realized I had no past criminal justice knowledge or experience whatsoever. In fact, I had never taken a criminal justice college course or related training in my life. What I found was I could be taught while on the job and quite a bit of training was offered typically. After a few months, I was promoted twice and moved into the position of Surveillance Officer (S.O.). An S.O. assists probation officers as they manage a group of adjudicated individuals who were court-ordered and placed on a probation caseload. I found the job interesting. I worked with many different people with diverse backgrounds. The one thing they had in common was they were convicted of a crime, usually a felony charge, and agreed to be placed on supervised probation. After a few years of being an S.O. and learning quite a lot, I decided to apply for Probation Officer. With a bachelor's degree, I was eligible. In 1994, I was promoted to Probation Officer (P.O.). A few years later, I transitioned to the Senior P.O. position. Working with convicted felons could be challenging and often exhausting. During my years as a supervising officer, I often felt I worked harder helping felons complete their court-ordered requirements than they did. As well-trained and armed, case-carrying peace officers, we had arrest authority over those whom we supervised. When a probationer repeatedly violated the conditions of their probation, it was not unusual for them to be handcuffed and transported to a county adult jail. I worked as a Probation Officer for twelve years. I always case-managed 60 to 70 people. It was fast-paced most days with rarely containing a dull moment – even the paperwork was intriguing. Four of the twelve years I supervised felons placed on Intensive Probation Supervision or I.P.S. It was a prison diversion program. If violated and sentenced by a judge, they were sent to prison. Even with help from an S.O., it was quite difficult to case manage twenty-five to thirty hard-core criminals. After fourteen years I was promoted to Unit Supervisor. I supervised eight to twelve officers managing their own caseloads. I transitioned well in the position and held the job for six years. Along the way, I learned to address human resources issues including those with progressive discipline. In 2011, I left the county department with twenty years of service. I applied and was hired as Chief Probation Officer for another Arizona county probation department. I held this administrative position for five years until 2016.

CHAPTER 10 FURTHER READING
ON LEADERSHIP

"Do nothing from selfish ambition or conceit, but in humility count others more significant than yourselves. – Philippians" - 2:3 ESV

At first, this sounds counter to what we'd consider good life advice, doesn't it? Do nothing out of ambition. The crux of the matter comes in the second half of the verse. In humility. Essentially, it's the humility part that I struggle most often with – and the reason I consider it counter to good life advice. I live my entire life in my own body, protecting it, feeding it, enjoy it for the most part. And yet, I am supposed to lead with a disregard for myself. The long and short of it? Yes.   Only by stepping outside ourselves, can we truly appreciate and lead in a godly manner. And the only way we can step outside ourselves is to grow in intimacy with God. Only by developing our relationship with Him, and understanding Him, can we allow God's intimacy to affect us – and create a place where we are okay with letting our own desires go. It is then that the desires of God overtake ours and we act in humility. We no longer crave ourselves. And, it is then, precisely, that we can be effective leaders for God in our work, our homes, and in our relationships.

CHAPTER 11

UNDYING LOVE

Many years had passed since the divorce from my daughter's mother, but I religiously made child support payments every two weeks, just as prescribed by the small-town southern Indiana judge. More than a decade removed the pain still consumed me at times. I had little to no contact with my firstborn daughter. I grieved the loss of a relationship with her greatly. What could I do to bring my daughter closer to me? I wanted her to know how much I loved and missed her. I lost out on precious years of her childhood. The sorrow was almost unbearable.

Her mother decided to leave our marriage, take our child away from me, and then filed for divorce. All I had left were unanswered questions. What could I do to show my daughter I was a different man than how my ex-wife described me? I had to take extreme action to overcome the loss – but it took enough healing to get to the place where I felt strong enough to do so.

I decided to file a petition for annual "out of state" visitation with my daughter with the court that had previously decided my custody case status. With no financial means for an attorney at the time, I represented myself in court. An initial hearing was granted and scheduled. I traveled from Arizona back to Indiana for my first hearing. My ex-father-in-law hired a lawyer to challenge my petition for two to four weeks of visitation in Arizona.

This renewed temporary custody and visitation battle was going to be difficult, if not impossible. In the midwestern community where the hearings took place, everyone was friends with or knew each other's family. This sort of good old boy network of friends and family in the local community created a close-knit albatross I would have to overcome. I was clearly the outsider. This was in no uncertain terms.

The assigned judge and local attorney representing my ex-wife likely dealt with one another quite often in court. This did not help my cause. I made three separate trips to southern Indiana to appear in court for three hearings. After the second hearing, and during the weekend I was there, I was granted an unsupervised day with my daughter.

At age 15, all my daughter knew about me was conjecture based on rumors or hearsay by others – not directly from me. Although the day was awkward, progress was made in my attempt for her to get to know me. I wanted her to know that dad, while absent for several reasons, was still a man who tried to be kind, and had the desire to be a loving father through this reconnection.

I feel like the plight of a dad is sometimes misunderstood when it comes to custody. As a father, I am supposed to be a financial supporter, a strength, and a sign of hope for my children. When the child or children are removed from his custody for any reason, any good-intended father struggles to comprehend how he can make a positive impact from a distance. I made mistakes and mistakes were made around me. This is the same for any dad. And it was the amalgamation of errors and misjudgments that led me to a place fathers often see: to make a seemingly hopeless decision that we don't want to but must. To be strong in the face of emotional pain, or be vulnerable and risk losing my identity as a man – at least that is what my less mature mind thought. Little did I know that I could be both vulnerable and strong at the same time. It is this complexity that allowed me to eventually connect with my daughter on a remedial level. It wasn't exactly what I had hoped at first, but it was a start.

When I returned for a third and final hearing, I was optimistic about the possibility of my child visitation petition being granted. However, upon leaving the lengthy hearing, I was deeply saddened by the court's ruling. During the hearing, testimony was provided by a juvenile therapist who was hired by the local attorney. The therapist interviewed my daughter at least twice. After the therapist interviewed me over the phone, she rendered a professional opinion: any out-of-state visitation would harm my daughter.

The judge also interviewed my daughter after reviewing the therapist's report. This was not a haphazard decision – yet still crushing. He came to the same conclusion. I was not granted visitation. In fact, the court decided to increase the amount of my twice-monthly child support payments. He ordered me to pay all my daughter's unpaid medical and dental expenses because my ex-wife said she couldn't pay them. The amount totaled over six thousand dollars.

In the end, I was allowed to see my daughter once more before I left town. Now at the young woman's age of fifteen, she told me to leave her alone. This memory still haunts me; it hurt tremendously. I felt an emptiness and betrayal. All my fears of being "incompetent" as a dad, or not good enough, would creep toward me like a slow, inevitable tide rising against the beach shore. I fought the hurt off if only to gain enough strength to continue the battle for custody rights. I knew in my heart my daughter could use a father's influence in her life – and guidance to help her manage her young, bright mind. I was not going to cease my efforts. This would only be a temporary delay in my mind.

CHAPTER 11 FUTHER READING
UNCONDITIONAL LOVE

"There is no fear in love. But perfect love drives out fear because fear has to do with punishment. The one who fears is not made perfect in love." – 1 John 4:18 ESV

How do you think about love? Do you look at the Hollywood version portrayed in the movies and think "That is the love I desire? Romantic, swept off my feet, always happy and always intimate." Or do you consider love a commitment - something that exists without reciprocity of feelings or security? Often our description of love stops at the former – and as a result, falls short of the love God desires we have for all: unconditional love. Why is that?

You'd be surprised but often our lack of deep understanding of love is because we fear. Fear of rejection. Fear of losing what we think we have. Fear of emotional vulnerability. Fear of accepting God's answer for love in favor of our won.

As you think about the love you have for others – a spouse, your friendships, colleagues, children - understand that if you fear losing something you cannot absolutely love them absolutely. Only by understanding that God provides all, are we able to accept that fear keeps us from growth, intimacy, and true affection for anyone or anything. It's a difficult proposition – and one that takes continued work – but somewhat attainable as we live out our days. The rewards of this type of love are beyond the scope of anything that Hollywood can adequately explain.

CHAPTER 12

THEY NEVER GIVE SOLE CUSTODY

TO A FATHER

I made the difficult decision to separate from the United States Air Force active duty after eleven years of military service. I moved from St. Louis, Missouri to southern Arizona and immediately sought full-time employment. I thought I might be able to join the 162nd Arizona Air National Guard. Although there were no jobs for an experienced air transportation supervisor, I was allowed to enlist as a traditional air guardsman. A one-weekend-a-month job wasn't enough to live independently or pay monthly bills. I began to look for what was familiar or full-time government employment. I pounded the pavement with a few possibilities after weeks of diligent job search. Finally, something did come my way. The county adult probation department had full-time entry-level jobs. I decided to apply. I was hired as a full-time Senior Clerk. Over the next twenty years, I was promoted to six positions including Surveillance Officer, Probation Officer, and Unit Supervisor. But for now, I had a full-time job with benefits. I was relieved. My son born in Alaska was now age five. His mother began to display behaviors which greatly concerned me after her return to the Arizona desert.

During the months that followed, the behavior became such a problem I questioned if I should continue the relationship for the sake of our child. My doubts prompted me to make the difficult decisions to separate, divorce, and petition the family courts for sole custody as a father. I knew this was something that rarely occurs. Judges usually allow mothers to maintain at least joint-parental custody status in child custody cases brought before them. Nonetheless, I moved forward with the information I believed might sway a court's opinion in my favor. Documented meetings with a past work supervisor regarding serious concerns about my wife's behavior occurring two years before the custody trial proved to be helpful. This documentation and other pertinent information were provided to the court. After a tumultuous three-day court trial, including witnesses testifying for both parties, a judge took my petition under advisement.

I was emotionally drained after my ex-wife's attorney attacked every aspect of my character. The deluge was his attempt to paint me as an unfit, irresponsible father. After a week, the court issued a decision. My attorney called me and I began to cry. Not tears of sorrow, but tears of pure joy. I was granted sole paternal child custody. Although I thought I had a good chance, I was still incredibly surprised. My lawyer told me I was fortunate. But like everything in life, there was a downside. I was ordered to pay my ex-wife's attorney fees. I already had to pay my own. Having to pay both perplexed me. Why would a judge grant a father full custody and order him to pay both parties' legal expenses? I would later make a deal with both lawyers whereby they would accept ten thousand dollars each, with no further claims to me. The most salient point was that I never lost sight of my goal. Perseverance and what I believe to be divine intervention got me the win.

CHAPTER 12 FUTHER READING
JUSTICE

"For the Lord loves justice;

he will not forsake his saints.

They are preserved forever,

but the children of the wicked shall be cut off."

-        Proverbs 37:28 ESV

I sometimes doubt what I believe. I question injustice in my life; I wonder if I can truly live in a world where I don't have to defend my own pride or my own opinion of what is right. But time and again, I realize that God does favor justice even when it doesn't result in the conclusion we want. The fact is, the godly person does seek justice according to his own standards at times. I know this because I do it myself. That is until I recognize the error of my ways and follow the truth that Jesus is the defender of truth and the only one who will find Justice.

It's a tall order for us to reflect in our everyday lives – but one that is paramount to our walk forward and in faith. To be able to believe and live in God's desire and His justice not our own is a freedom we cannot experience otherwise.

PART TWO: PRAIRIE HOME COMPANION

THE FASCINATING THING ABOUT FASCINATING THINGS

Different and similar at the exact same time, stories are all about perspectives. While it's said there are only seven stories in the world – boy meets girl, girl meets boy, boy loses girl, and so on – there are an infinite number of combinations that add flavor, moxie, or sadness to any plot. The genesis of lasting impressions is something that's often misunderstood though. Why are some stories more fascinating than others? Is it because they are horrible, thus making us feel better afterward after the adrenaline wears off? Maybe. Is it because we are thankful the story didn't happen to us? Likely. Is it because we find that the truth is like our own truth, our own situation, our lot in life, in some irreducibly complex way?

The fascinating thing about fascinating things is that we don't mind learning about them from a distance – from the safety of a "visitor only" point of view. It is enormously, even improbably difficult to be fascinated by something that hits too close to home due to the potential horror, trauma, or depravity we might see in ourselves.

Ultimately, the fascinating thing about fascinating things is they are usually about us – whether we like it or not. The distance to our specific situation allows us to either endure, persevere, or crumble under the pressure.

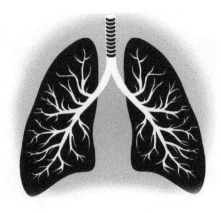

CHAPTER 13

THE LUNG-DISEASED MOTHER AND
PARTIALLY DEAF FATHER

During my youth in the late 1960s and early 1970s, people treated disabilities with less respect and empathy than today. My mother was born in 1924 and had a fitful and repeated cough that lingered a lifetime. When she coughed deeply or at length her diseased lungs would release horrible things into the surroundings and displeased those around her. The glares and unfavorable treatment she often received were not pleasant – especially for her child to adsorb. The resultant emotional effect codified itself in several ways with my mother. She lacked self-esteem and had little confidence in things. She attempted to live a normal life, attending preparatory school, and graduating high school.

My father was born a premature fraternal twin. His sister did not survive birth. They were three pounds each and he was placed in a shoe box until he gained weight and strength. Born in 1918 there was nothing available to help premature babies survive. The result he had was partial hearing loss in both of his ears. He was the oldest of six children and the other five had no known impairments. My father was cast aside by nonempathic parents because of this disability. They loved him but often did not know what to do or say to him. He later regretted not attending a deaf and blind school. Going to a special school was not encouraged, and he was afraid to leave home to attend a school many miles away. He would receive his first pair of hearing aids at age twenty-one. He was so grateful for them. But the damage to his education and a shaky start to life had already rooted itself in his fragile young mind. The lack of education and the loss of normal youthful years that help mature a child was torture for many years and persisted into adulthood. He was the target of many kids growing up and, if possible, even more adults as he became a man, who thought it odd that he could not hear.

It really hurt him – and me.

Watching both my mother and father navigate life when I was a child was difficult. A "normal" childhood finds kids looking at their parents with reverence, and often finding comfort and appeal as they consider their parents sometimes heroic figures. Who has not felt their parents knew the answers to everything growing up – whether true or not? I was robbed of that security early in life.

My overall opinion of people suffered. But my sympathy and empathy for those with disabilities grew significantly. Little could I have known my third child, now an adult, would be born with cerebral palsy. Becoming a father of a child with disabilities has provided me with a unique perspective. My willingness to accept others with medical or physical issues developed at a youthful age. The downside was this perspective helped mold me into an enabler of sorts, and why I made key decisions that later had a negative impact upon so many years of my life.

There is no way around it: my parents loved and raised me the best they could. My father was a custodian and my mother was a homemaker. We had little money and lived modestly. This instilled within me a driving desire to succeed in whatever I chose to do. My parents did not understand that facet of their parenting. Upon reflection, it did not matter they did not understand because I did.

CHAPTER 13 FURTHER READING

TRIBULATION

"Rejoice in hope, be patient in tribulation, be constant in prayer. "

– Romans 12:12 ESV

I've learned that my experience of overcoming pain is a three-step process many times. First, I must remember that I will have trials and difficulties in life. God promises it in his Word. He says nothing different. So, I have to have great patience to endure the hardships that come my way.

I have to remember that my hope is in Christ – nothing else. And because of this hope, I know that whatever happens my best interests are at the Heart of my Savior and Lord. To not have hope in Christ is to not believe in Christ. There may be moments where we doubt – but never moments of complete abandonment.

Finally, I have to be in constant prayer about the difficulties I have in life. When I do so I know that I am staying close to God – not myself. By prayer, I submit my issues, my worries, and my concerns to His plan.

Following the three steps outlined in Romans 12:12, I not only follow God's instruction, but I also know that His instruction won't come back empty. He will give me patience, the hope, and the prayers to not only go through any challenges but to accept what he has for me on the other side, regardless of the outcome.

Yes, my parents endured a lot of heartache and pain – physical and emotional – and I too encountered significant trauma. But any encounter is dampened and I can find peace in the midst of it, because of who God is.

CHAPTER 14

THE STRUGGLE

I remember watching from my bedroom window, amazed as my father slowly brush-painted our station wagon in our grass-covered backyard. I could see the heavy strokes of paint, laden one upon another as my dad hitched his pants up so we could squat lower and get to the bottom of the car doors and body. I wondered why we could not take our car to an autobody shop where it could be properly spray painted. I know other families had done so in order to give their cars a new look, or a fresh appeal. I felt a strange but definite melancholy grow over me as the obvious answer entered my mind. It was a truth I didn't comprehend until that moment. We were poor.

I have many related stories that involve money, or more accurately, our usual lack of. It was difficult to watch my parents financially struggle week by week, month by month, and year by year as I grew older. At first, I did not think anything of it. I was a child with little concept of being less fortunate than others. But as I matured, the light shown on our financial plight brightly. I became self-conscious about it.

My father was a custodian and my mother could not work. There was not much left after monthly bills are paid and basic grocery needs were met. These circumstances were not without cause. My father was born hearing-impaired. He did not have an opportunity to learn to read, express himself on paper, or accomplish much in the way of basic math. The lack of education would remind him – and us – of its detriment his entire life. My mother, a high school graduate, did help my father to learn different, beneficial things that helped. They both did the best they could for each other to "keep things going" to survive.

They did not get along wonderfully when I was younger. The struggle was commonplace. Back then, I was not certain if the lack of relationship bliss stemmed from the financial deficits, or if the verge of financial ruin exacerbated the relationship failings. Today, I would imagine it was equal parts from both. When it mattered most, though – when they had to get through a new challenge financially, emotionally, or physically – somehow, they would batten down the hatches, and work as a team. Their joint effort to survive financially during tough times inspired me. It taught me how to overcome my own struggles in life and what I did and did not want to do with money.

Usually, there was no savings account to draw upon for any financial emergencies. With a low credit score, my parents were forced to obtain money by whatever legal means. They never broke laws, but survival was often attained by whatever possible. They would secure loans from high-interest loan companies who specialized in those with poor credit scores and low incomes. It was not unusual for loan interest rates to be as high as twenty-five percent. After securing several of these loans, my parents were heavily in debt. All they could do was pay the interest on each loan every month. I would later refer to the loan companies as legal loan sharks. To be fair, no one forced this upon them. But they could never get ahead. Their indebtedness was not caused by drinking, drug use, or gambling addictions. Just not enough income coming in each month to cover normal household expenses. It was worrisome.

Eventually, an inheritance from my father's parents paid off all their debt. They were free from their overwhelming debts after many years of financial woe. As a younger child and then teenager, all the duress was difficult for me to figure out at first. Over the years, I witnessed enough of it that I learned what I did not want to do later in life.

It is common across all societies in our country or world to experience money problems, but we were living below the poverty level. This had a profound impact on me psychologically and emotionally. It prompted me to become a "saver." As an adult, I told myself I would work hard and not fall victim to the same circumstances. But that is not the entirety of the story, is it?

Sure, people struggle with finances. They always have and they always will. But when I reflect and dig a little deeper, a clearer picture comes to mind. I loved my parents – they were what I knew growing up. They were home, they were safe, and they were what I as a child could lean on when I did not know what else to lean on. To realize the destitution with which we lived – and compare it to other families, other people – that is what struck me the hardest. Like the health issues my parents faced, I felt the world had dealt them a raw deal before I was born. My mother and father were given a lump of coal for Christmas that kept on giving. And the only respite from the continued challenges they faced came by chance, not by their own hand. They could not dig themselves out of life's circumstances. They were not capable of making a "comfortable" life.

I was not embarrassed. It was something different. Something more subtly rooted in motivation for my future. I may have even been scared. What I do know is that I did not want to suffer, and I felt sad for my parents who did. The desire to avoid similar circumstances would be something that would later drive me to do surprising things in life as I searched for security.

CHAPTER 14 FURTHER READING
THE STRUGGLE

"But he said to me, "My grace is sufficient for you, for my power is made perfect in weakness." Therefore, I will boast all the more gladly of my weaknesses, so that the power of Christ may rest upon me. For the sake of Christ, then, I am content with weaknesses, insults, hardships, persecutions, and calamities. For when I am weak, then I am strong." - 2 Corinthians 12:9-10 ESV-

It is a quandary, really. When I encounter struggle, I can either pull away from my faith or grow closer to it. What is the difference? I believe part of it has to do with the fact that I get consumed by the obstacles in front of me. I focus on how great the power of something bigger than me feels and lose sight of the truth. In my life, I walk further from God because I forget who He is and the promises He has made in my life. I don't remember that He has promised He is with me and ever grieves for me in my sadness and struggles.

I grow stronger when I embrace Him and understand that His ways are greater than mine. He has overcome the world and I simply need to let go of my fears and walk with Him – or if need be – let Him carry me. There is comfort in knowing that God personally, specifically, watches over me, waiting for the opportunity to take care of my worries.

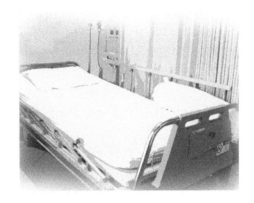

CHAPTER 15

TWENTY-EIGHT DAYS SHORT

The hospice nurse asked me, plainly, without emotion: "Is he still breathing? Is he still alive?"

"I'm not sure," I replied.

I had spent the past week and a few nights watching my father take his last breaths on earth. My father passed away on the same day the nurse asked. He lived a full life at eighty-nine years, eleven months & two days. Twenty-eight days short of his 90th birthday.

When my mother passed at age sixty-nine, in June 1994,

I was not ready for it. Who really is ever ready for the decisiveness of death? Especially a parent whose death often reveals mortality is right around the corner. When October 2008 came, and my father lay still in his room with the matter-of-fact, questioning nurse, I was more mature and I think, prepared.

After moving from Indiana to Arizona in the early nineties, my mother lived only two more years. I've always felt that the drastic and significant move she made to the desert in extremely poor health exacerbated the downward trajectory of her final days. My father took good care of her those two years as her health declined even more rapidly. Nobody would expect a forty-five-year marriage to always be pleasant – and in fact, there were days that were more knock down and drag out than they were filled with picturesque "love" for my parents. He truly loved her, though, in a way many men don't love their spouse. He was committed and did the best he could for my mother when it seemingly mattered the most. I loved him for that.

The subsequent fourteen years my father and I had together after my mother's passing was a blessing and a true gift from God. We inched closer as I learned how to relate to him differently than when I was younger. I use the term closer because when I was younger, our relationship was more distant than any other attribute. My father was more a figurehead than a dad when I was young, and an absent one at that – emotionally and physically. When present, he usually lacked compassion. This had a tremendous impact upon me.

My father always worked for more than he related to his family. Whether it was a custodial job, remodeling homes, fishing, or time in his carpentry shop creating masterpieces of wood wizardry he would try to sell in craft shows and bazaars, there was little quality time left over to spend with my mother or me. He never took me to public parks or played catch with me. No activities involving just the two of us. I honestly believe he didn't understand how to be that father. The man who cultivates a relationship to improve the life of their children or spouse in ways other than providing food and shelter. I didn't blame him – I felt bad for him. Such simple concepts were not really bestowed upon my father by my always hardworking grandfather either. His model wasn't caring, affection, or quality time. There wasn't room for relationships when the primary objective of life was accomplishment, vis-à-vis work. My father was taught that caring for his family meant working, making money, and putting a meal on the table. In that order, and in large part, to that extent. It was simply all he had been taught and knew. What money my father did make wasn't for the sake of making money, though. His focus on work and money wasn't in a selfish or greedy way.

I was often told I was his unpaid laborer when we tore down houses to get free lumber, or if I was helping with a remodeling project. In its most basic sense, I was a work slave, as he was to his own father. As I got older, I eventually became tired of being this unpaid laborer. So, as a matter of course, I resented him. Those were my memories of my father when my mother died.

After my mother died, my father's physical health, and "fighting, hard-working" spirit slowed. Pieces of him were displaced, and shards of his life had gone missing after mom was gone. His state of mind noticeably changed. He became less intense. He softened. Things like caring and compassionate started to creep out of the cracks of his frayed soul. I felt as if I was given a second chance to know and love him.

My two sons had great times with their grandfather.

Sadly, due to timing, my daughter did not. My father, sons and I did many things together during those fourteen years. It was a time in my life I cherish as I continue to grow older myself. I don't know if it was really that good or if memories are colored differently by time and healing, but undeniably, my father wouldn't have changed had my mother not left too soon in her life. In a way then, I can thank my mother – in her leaving us, she left us with a better man – and blessed us one last time.

From age seventy-six to eighty-eight, my father built a woodworking shop with the last vestiges of his hard work ethic and became a favorite of his circle of friends, including a few lady friends over the years who helped care for him, and about him, as his life wound down. He filled the shop with tools he needed to make a myriad of different birdhouses, dollhouses, pieces of furniture, stools, benches, woodcuts of desert plants and animals, Christmas ornaments, and any other number of things. He was even featured in the Arizona Daily Star, a local city newspaper on August 11, 2005, for his talented woodworking skills.

Time stands still for no one. He finally quit driving his car in his late eighties, moved out of his home, and liquidated an extensive woodworking shop. He moved into some low-income government-subsidized apartments that allowed only limited space for him to live. He then developed and died from leukemia a year later. He lived a mixed life with good and bad. But upon further reflection, his life wasn't short twenty-eight days of anything. He lasted long enough to encounter challenges, accomplishments, the joy of children, the agony of loss, and the sprinkling of redemption. What a life he lived.

There is a Korean proverb that says a man cries only three times in his life. He cries when he is born. He cries when his mother dies, and a man cries when he loses his country. I miss my father – I can't think about him without tears welling up in my eyes. I wonder. Are the tears I want to cry for him, my mother, or for me?

CHAPTER 15 FURTHER READING

LOSS

"Blessed are those who mourn, for they shall be comforted."
- Matthew 5:4 ESV

It is difficult to see the joy in grief, to see life in loss. And yet, that is exactly what God asks me to see. He talks in Scripture about rejoicing in tribulation and finding peace in the loss. He asks me to let go of the world so that I might find myself in Him. How is this possible – the instruction runs counter to every way of the world.

That is the point though. God is separate from the ways of the world – and if I really trust in His word, I know He will be there with me. You see, God doesn't stop at asking me to find joy, He also tells me how to find it. He says He will comfort me. And I will be blessed.

The encouragement from Jesus is real despite how much I don't want to understand it. His love for me, for you, is greater than the love we understand and he desires to share it with us every day.

CHAPTER 16

THE MIRACLE BABY

I hung up the phone, crying. A call I had anticipated finally came. My mother had died at a senior nursing care facility. In June 1994, I was thirty-six years old. I was sad I was not with her when she passed. I had visited her with my young son two days prior. But, with my busy life, a demanding job, and family responsibilities, I failed to visit her more frequently in her final days. The circumstances haunt me still.

At the age of sixty-nine, my mother had lived longer than many expected during a period of time when less advanced medication and treatment were available to her. Those who were surprised at her stamina, included the numerous doctors who had cared for her during her truncated lifetime. At a very young age - after a series of left and right lung-related ailments - my mother told me her body developed a permanent lung disease called bronchiectasis. It is a serious form of bronchitis whereby the lungs can be in a perpetual infected state due to their weakened condition. Pouches form in the lungs and infection after infection can riddle the lungs for a lifetime. While today, with regular treatment, a normal life expectancy can be attained, it's only through exhaustive treatments. Regardless of the case, the infections prompt the afflicted to cough up phlegm consistently, many times each day. That's a lasting memory of mom, coughing. Phlegm. Her constant physical struggle.

As a result of her affliction, mom was in a sickly condition for most of her life. This was furthered when she gave birth to me. She often told me that for me to be born without inheriting her malady, the obstetrician required she have her lungs frequently pumped. This would remove any infected fluid build-up and lessen the chances of my poor health. The process was painful and uncomfortable, but it did, for all intents and purposes, keep me from inheriting this horrific disease. I would not have the shortness of breath and weakened health my mother would learn to live with. She told me proudly, and often, I was her "miracle baby," which was probably echoed by her doctors.

Mom's health condition had a significant impact on her psyche and emotional state in everyday life. She often lacked confidence and self-esteem. She did try to maintain a positive attitude, although it was difficult for her. She soldiered on through - for her benefit and mine. Throughout her life, my mother maintained a sense of caring and empathy for others. It was one of her strongest character traits.

That didn't mean mom was able to overcome all the outcomes of her sickly state. She would become emotional and depressed at times. Depression and sadness were something she shared with an older and younger sister (my aunts). Mom had three other sisters who died at an early age due to childhood diseases with no cures at the time. Like my father, she had a temper which also prompted many disagreements and arguments with dad. Both mom and dad ran the gambit of emotional and physical distresses in their marriage – it's an absolute wonder they lasted as long as they did, despite it all.

Not surprisingly, many of these character traits my parents exhibited, I also share. It's as if they have bequeathed these gifts upon me as an inheritance, rather than money or other riches. Instead, I got their anger, depression, emotional hurdles (high and low), and occasional challenges to my self-esteem. While I don't blame my family for specifically giving me these characteristics, I do understand the nature of the influence the emotional battles had on me as a youngster and how they have affected my make-up and character as an adult.

The choices I have made in my life, whether they be good or bad, were not determined by my parents, their maladies, their emotional intelligence, or lack thereof. But the choices I have made, and my reactions to them most certainly were modeled to me as a youth. And, for better or worse, my ability or inability to respond correctly was trained into me to a certain extent. How could it not be? A child only knows what he sees. To break free, then, is a matter of fortitude, decision, and change. All of it over time, none of it, instantly. Regardless, I embrace who I am, faults and all, as they have reminded me of things my mother said or did. One of my biggest takeaways from her difficult life was her courage to keep going even when she often did not feel like it. I was fortunate to get additional time with my dad – not so lucky with mom. Almost thirty years after my mother's passing, I certainly cherish what time I was blessed to have with her. She taught me so much in so many ways.

I think this may have been mom's greatest success. Her lasting impression and teachings that encouraged me to be who I am today – a man who seeks after God, who cares for his kids, and who writes truthfully, with love about his life and the lives of his parents. She impacted people more than she knew.

CHAPTER 16 FURTHER READING
AFFLICTION

"For this light momentary affliction is preparing for us an eternal weight of glory beyond all comparison, as we look not to the things that are seen but to the things that are unseen. For the things that are seen are transient, but the things that are unseen are eternal." - 2 Corinthians 4:17-18 ESV

I often neglect God's Word in favor of my own understanding. I lean on my own perspectives of the world and the truths I deem appropriate based on my experiences and call it a day. Unfortunately, I am delusional if this is the way to manage my life. The book of Darrell (while I'm sure has merit) pales in comparison to the book of God.

The book that I am writing focuses on experience to develop truth. If something favorable happens, then I tend to think it is more truthful. If something negative takes place, I hope it's not truthful. If I have a good time then things are great, and a bad time spells struggle.

God's book is different. His book remains steady

regardless of circumstance, experience, or situation. If things are unfavorable, His word is still true. If situations are good, His word is still true. Nothing changes in God's word based on feelings, environment, or people. It is because of this unchanging nature and character of God that I can find stability in what is real rather than the lack of foundation I can find in my own worries.

I encourage you to find stability and foundation in God so that your joy, peace, and love are unaffected to great extent. It is much more satisfying and helpful to manage the afflictions of life in such a way.

CHAPTER 17

PAIN, REFLECTION AND NEW BEGINNINGS

In 1999, I became depressed. It was difficult to deny the truth of my life over the past twenty years. From May 1979 to May 1999, I married three women and subsequently divorced three times. It was a punch to the gut that got no better the more I considered it, the clearer it became. Instead, the truth sent me down a railway of what felt like incompetence and guilt – where the train only stopped at failed marriage after failed marriage. The center of it all: how did I get to the point where I legitimately thought I was ready to have a life-long partner (which I honestly did) and then found my way to a complete and total reversal of that opinion?

To take my mind off the landmine of emotional destruction and stop staring the truth in the face for too long, I threw myself deeply into my job. While immersing myself in probation work, I also decided to enroll in a graduate degree program. Another diversion. Why contemplate the turbulent realities of my past when I could submerge myself in education, work, and "personal growth," or, as some like to call it – avoidance?

I took a break from any type of romantic relationship for two years. This allowed me time to think and heal. I told myself I would never marry again. I just was not good at it. Turns out monogamy was not my cup of tea either. When it came to marital affairs, I lived through many difficulties – and as stated earlier – several failed marriages. But the one thing I still was, and always would be, was a risk taker in relationships. Especially when it came to female relationships. Sure, all relationships carry a certain amount of risk, vulnerability, and emotional exposure to gain trust, love, and "place" with the other person. My relationships were different though. It was as if the inextricable, predominant trait of my romantic relationships was the risk itself. Not a means to an end, but the end.

Rolling the dice at the matrimonial craps table was something I was familiar, almost comfortable, with despite its tragic turns. In December 2001, I asked a friend to have dinner with me. We were just close friends prior to this night but afterward, something had changed. This woman was different, and I was drawn to her. After all that had occurred in my past, I was reticent to put my heart out there again. Would I really risk another relationship? After understanding my allude to risk, after knowing my common trajectory in relationships, and after understanding that history might be the best indicator of my future, was I really considering a new romantic partner?

After many conversations and time spent together, we decided to see where things could go. I could not believe I was going down this path again. As our relationship evolved, we began to have feelings for one another that ran much deeper than dating or casual friendship – even romantically. I suggested we wait at least five years before we ever considered getting truly serious as a couple. She thought this was a good idea. I told her if she did not like what she saw or heard during this period she could and should walk away.

From my perspective, although ending the relationship might hurt me terribly, it certainly would be better than starting what could be another failed marriage. I simply could not take another one. Not emotionally, physically, spiritually, or financially. So, we tread lightly.

Five years passed. I completed my master's degree with a co-worker who attended the same courses. Together we decided to apply to and were eventually accepted into a doctoral degree program. During this incredibly special time, I worked full-time at a demanding probation officer job, attended night classes, raised kids, paid child support, maintained a home for my family, and attempted to have some semblance of a social life with my cautious romantic interest. When I reflected upon these years, I honestly do not know how it all happened. My mid-forties to early fifties were a magical time. In 2006, I graduated with a doctorate in education, began teaching criminal justice evening courses part-time at a local university, was promoted to the position of Probation Unit Supervisor at work, and moved into a new home. And, most importantly, I got married for a fourth, and last, time.

CHAPTER 17 FURTHER READING
SEASONS

"For everything there is a season, and a time for every matter under heaven." - Ecclesiastes 3:1 ESV

I try to forget difficulties of the past but one of the more absurd behaviors I can do is hold onto the past with equally as tight a grip, both emotionally and mentally. It is as though I feel I lose a part of myself if I lose past trauma. Without those horrible experiences am I really who I say I am? Without the hurt what was the point? It is a valid process for rationalizing my past, but it's not the complete picture. I am made up of all the experiences I have but they don't solely define me.

In a strange twist of fate, the notion that we find identity in trauma or loss is a sad reality. The fact that we may have poured so much into someone else, or a different event – and then to lose it – causes us such grief. It is tantamount to establishing who we are as a person. If we lose a grasp of what happened, we lose a part of ourselves. Did we really exist if that pain or grief is lost?

Many people have said that when they accepted Christ as their savior, their testimony was lesser if there wasn't trauma in their lives – a black-to-white contrast. Yes, the challenges of sin in our lives can derail us and add color to our witness when we come to Christ as a child of God. But our sin isn't the full story. We shouldn't glorify our sin. Instead, we should glorify God. It is the redemption of man that is the important part of our salvation, not the sin. God is so clear about this concept that He says he wipes away every sin. We are born anew every single day.

The fact is, there is a season for everything in our lives. There are times of good and times of bad. There are difficulties and there are periods where we overcome whatever is set in front of us. Through it all, the hurts, the sin, the redemption, and change is the common denominator until our days end. How we view those changes and move forward will dictate our ability to find peace in the face of them.

My encouragement is that we should not linger in the past, the loss, or the grief we encounter in our lives. It is important to recognize what happened. It is important to understand that everything we do or that happens to us adds to our story. But our past does not define us, our future does. If you are a child of God, his future is hope, not focused on the past. His future is a perfect restoration of who you should be - in a glorious body, with Him forever.

CHAPTER 18

THE WEEKEND WARRIOR

When you think of a weekend warrior, you might think about the middle-aged man who is a regular joe during the week, then dons shorts, a t-shirt, and athletic shoes as he goes a few rounds on the basketball courts or playing pickleball. It is as though a weekend warrior is reduced to a man who seeks out glory on weekends because the week is too full of responsibility. The weekend warrior is living a dream on the weekends, reality Monday through Friday.

One of the most difficult decisions I ever made during my forty-five paid work years was whether to remain on

U. S. Air Force active duty or to separate with an Honorable Discharge. In July 1992, I did decide to leave with nearly eleven years of total service. However, my plan was to join the 162nd Fighter Wing, Arizona Air National Guard (ANG), and secure full-time work. That way I could still be within the military, just differently. My plan didn't work. However, I did join in Sept. 1992 as a traditional guardsman, or as full-timers called us, weekenders.

Weekend ANG positions were all that were available for what I was trained to do. I made the best of it, and eventually found a full-time job that I'd spend with county government for the following twenty years. When I was active duty, I didn't like when air guard staff were temporarily assigned to my work area. In general, they usually didn't know what they were doing. Most of the time, they got in the way of our accomplishing the mission. But my opinion changed dramatically after I became one of them. I realized quickly that part-time military personnel were just trying to get required training completed. These weekend warrior positions were the only way they could. Part-time military service was different than what I envisioned. It was difficult because I was expected to complete all my training while already working full-time somewhere else. This I found to be no easy task.

My first assignment was to the base civil engineering unit. I organized tools and did inventory. Within six months, I was reassigned to base supply. I attended military school in San Antonio, Texas. It took me away from my full-time adult probation department job, but I still completed all required training while working full-time. I really didn't enjoy the supply work, but it did provide me with a job on the air guard base. I worked at base supply one weekend a month for a few years when a new job came along. It was similar to my active-duty work. This base logistics specialist position was as close as I would ever get. Once again, I attended another out-of-state military training school. This one was near Denver, Colorado. After I completed the required training, I was back to doing what I enjoyed with those I enjoyed doing it with.

The talented organization planners I worked with organized and facilitated all air travel for base personnel. The largest and most complex event we put together every year was a two-week trip to Hawaii. Our ANG F-16 fighter planes flew to Hawaii to conduct pilot training exercises. They were refueled during their flights by KC-135 tanker planes. We called them flying gas stations. After fighter pilots took off, their planes did not touch another runway until arriving in Hawaii. This was a well-coordinated operation. We were responsible for ensuring all deployed base staff had hotel rooms, meals, and transportation. Arranging entertainment such as a traditional beach Hawaiian luau with a buried roasted pig and hula dancers were a part of our many duties while on the trip. It was considerable work, but I enjoyed all these experiences. The two weeks flew by. Soon we were wrapping up and returning to base. In Sept. 1998, after over six great years as a weekend warrior after my almost eleven years of active duty, I officially retired from further military service. What a ride it was.

CHAPTER 18 FURTHER READING

WORK

"Whatever you do, work heartily, as for the Lord and not for men," - Corinthians 3:23 ESV

In a world that relishes accomplishment and achievement, it is easy to revel in the glory bestowed upon high-performing workers. The rewards of finishing projects on time, saving a company money, or completing a task under strict guidelines and rules are many. People slap your back; they smile and they say "congrats!" Maybe as in the eighties and nineties, you received a toaster as a bonus. If you are even more fortunate, you would get financial recompense for the exhaustive hours you put in, toiling away. Usually not something that occurs with government employment. There are some exceptions. But that is where the recognition ends, isn't it? Once you walk away, it's on to the next project. What have you done for me, lately?

There is nothing wrong with accomplishment. Even greater, however, is to know that any accomplishment can be done with the Lord in mind. By shifting our focus of work to provide glory for Jesus, we know that whether we get applause from men or not, we are doing a great job. So long as our efforts are true, wise, and for His benefit, then any work is amazing work. And the congratulations? It will come when we go to heaven with these hopeful words "Well done, good and faithful servant." There can be no greater congratulations.

CHAPTER 19

SHOULD I STAY OR SHOULD I GO

On May 19, 1976, I graduated with honors from an old historic high school located in a rural area of southern Indiana. Located on a country road, it was surrounded by corn and soybean fields. My parents who had attended the graduation ceremony planned a celebration at our home. I was expected to attend. Many invited family and friends assembled to help celebrate my academic achievement and wish me well. I was leaving for college soon. My future now awaited me.

Little did my parents and others know that this graduate had made other plans for the evening. My friend and fellow classmate planned to attend a huge party with our fellow graduates and we were invited. After my parent's house party was fully underway, my friend arrived in his awesome Chevy Camaro. He honked the horn signaling it was time to leave for the much cooler graduation party.

My parents had concerns that there will be alcohol, marijuana, and other drugs at the grad party. They didn't want their son anywhere near that situation. As an argument ensued, my mother's numerous emotional comments were made to make me feel guilty and to not leave a house full of people who came there for me. This placed me in a no-win situation. As my friend continued to impatiently honk, I eventually made my way to his Camaro to tell him I would not be going with him as we had planned. The prevailing thought in my mind was that I didn't want to disappoint my disabled older parents.

Ultimately, feelings of guilt coupled with some resentment overcame me. I started to become angry. As I walked to my friend's car, each step I took in my walk of shame quickly turned to embarrassment as I informed him I wouldn't be joining him that night. This generated a saddened look of disbelief and disgust from my long-time friend. The expression on his face as he pulled away along with my feelings of manipulation, having given in to my parents, haunted me for many years.

What could have been for me that night? That was the question that circled my mind for an eternity. After 47 years, the events of that evening are as memorable and fresh for this now older man as the evening they all occurred. As I reflect on the experience, I've thought about what it would have been like to celebrate at a party with my fellow graduates. Would I have safely returned home later that night or the following morning? Would I have fallen victim to serious injury resulting from a car crash caused by a friend's riskless driving?

In other words, were the actual events of this evening to my benefit or detriment? These answers will never be provided. As we usually want what we can't have, these circumstances over the passing years have provided me with some fascination. Other people may think it's a ridiculous story. Over the passing years, I have recounted this scenario many times and some have thought it unfortunate. Others not so much. After much contemplation and reflection, I now think it's actually a story about loyalty versus desire. An absolute teachable moment.

Youthful decisions made in haste during heated moments

are often left with sadness, guilt, and regret. This grad night party scenario and the circumstances surrounding it have served as a much-discussed cautionary tale. It's interesting how just a few moments in a person's life can have such an impact as we grow older. Whether perceived as important or not, this and many other life events help mold us as individuals. It's simply one of God's ways of teaching us lessons for life.

CHAPTER 19 FUIRTHER READING
DAILY BREAD

"I am the living bread that came down from heaven. If anyone eats of this bread, he will live forever. And the bread that I will give for the life of the world is my flesh." – John 6:51 ESV

How does someone grow closer to God every day? My attempt to grow closer begins and ends with two things. First, I recognize who God is for all His greatness, His spectacular character, His grace, His mercy, and His love for me and all mankind. Second, I know that the more I spend time with him the more I will be fed. Christ is our daily bread – He feeds us spiritually, mentally, and emotionally. If we can grow intimate with Him, then we can see his truths and live them even more.

I know personally, I am lost in the dark and I see His light far away. But with every step I take towards that light, the more I see, the more I understand. The same is true for everyone. And, as we get closer to His life, and grow more intimate, the more we can reflect on who He is in our daily lives. His daily bread is sufficient. Let's eat of it every day.

As I recall the story about my graduation night, I can't help to notice how God was providing me with daily bread that I didn't see for years to come. He was giving me insight and wisdom that would help me see how myopic my view was. Was that singular party really that important in the scheme of things? The answer is no. The world got so much bigger, and so much better, than missing a party. This was what God reached out to me with – but what I refused to see. It is moments like this that make me appreciate just how much God feeds us, whether we accept it or not.

CHAPTER 20

GREAT TEACHERS

I had the privilege of knowing great teachers while attending junior high and high school at the beginning of the seventies. The teachers encouraged me to do more with my life. They spurred me to move forward, rather than remain in a small community and work at one of many local factories. At times, as a group, they were not folks I would have necessarily listened to or sought after for advice. Because of a strong bond and mutual trust though, I found myself listening more. I became good friends with a few of them. The lessons I learned from teachers were immeasurable. Teachers, as a group, are usually never paid their worth. Great teachers do not instruct others hoping to receive great compensation. They instruct youth because it feeds their soul. One "critical path" decision I made was based on encouragement to seek out and attend higher education courses. Doing so enhanced my life and provided other opportunities later in life I would not have anticipated.

Although my parents had no problem with me going to college, they did not necessarily understand the decision either. Our family was considered lower income during my years leading to college, so I received educational grants along with scholarships I had earned from my good grades. I still can picture my mother's face when she came with me to my chosen community college. After meeting with financial aid and admissions staff, I was told college tuition, my meals, and housing expenses would all be paid. It was an absolute miracle. My mother began to understand my desire to move on with my life.

My parents certainly wanted the best for me, but I am not

sure they really understood what that would be, or could be, for that matter. Time spent with good mentors helped me find out more about myself. Even to this day, I seek good mentors, and to be a good mentor to others when given the chance – or choice. A good mentor relationship can empower a person with confidence. Great teachers and mentors may not realize the positive impact they have on the students they influence. It's been so many years and I have not forgotten about the impact that a couple of teachers made in my life. In the absence of a strong parent or another positive role model, teachers can have an influence in the lives of students who are lucky to have them.

CHAPTER 20 FURTHER READING
TEACHERS

"Not many of you should become teachers, my brothers, for you know that we who teach will be judged with greater strictness. For we all stumble in many ways. And if anyone does not stumble in what he says, he is a perfect man, able also to bridle his whole body." – James 3:1-2 ESV

As I reflect on the wonderful teachers in my life, I can feel the weight of their charge. But I realize it is not theirs alone. We are all teachers in some part of our life. I taught others about my experiences in law enforcement. During my years as a Unit Supervisor & Chief Probation Officer, I taught many how to perform better at their employment. I instructed my children about the ways of the world when they were younger and today. I pray I've taught my wife that I love her dearly.

As I read the Bible, though, I gain knowledge, and that knowledge I impart to others – cautiously, lest I fail to remark upon it correctly. Teaching God's word is the greatest type of instructing for a man or woman. To share the Good News carefully, precisely, and enthusiastically is a wonderful, beautiful thing. But this teaching must be done with the utmost steady hand, ensuring it is not glibly tossed about. People's lives are at stake and teaching them the correct things of God is paramount to glorifying God, stewarding his principles, and providing a helpful path so people can understand more about His saving grace.

CHAPTER 21

THE BIG KAHUNA

In January 2011, after working as a Unit Supervisor for five years, I decided I needed more. More responsibility, more challenges, and more wages than my current position was providing. With support from department management, I began to inquire about Chief Probation Officer (CPO) vacancies across 15 counties in Arizona. As positions became available, I started to apply for them. After interviewing a few times and not being selected, I learned how to better interview. I gained more confidence along the way. Some family or friends didn't share this confidence in my ability to become a CPO. I was repeatedly asked, "Why are you doing this?" Why wasn't I content with the job and life I had. These people didn't understand my driven desire to do more with my life. Throughout my life when folks have said no, I said yes. This was engrained within me from a young age. It's all I knew how to be. I was comfortable with going against the odds. Sometimes I won, sometimes I lost, but I gave it everything I had. As time passed, a county 300 miles away or five driving hours was seeking a new Chief P.O. I asked my wife if I should apply. She said yes. By now I was much more confident believing I could do what was expected. My years as a supervisor prepared me for more responsibility. I was approved for an interview so I made the long drive, preparing the night before at a nearby motel. When entering the morning interview, I noted there were many in the room. The questions were what I expected. I ended the interview advising the panel I was "the logical choice." If selected they would not regret it. Afterward, I was confident. Human resources called and requested I return for the follow-up conversation. I was one of three applicants. The three of us toured department facilities that included a juvenile detention center I would be responsible for and to operate and staff. Although the process was a little awkward, I got through it all with no concerns. I returned home with much anticipation. When several days passed with no response, I became concerned. I asked my supervisor what he thought. He said no news meant they were still considering me. Be patient. Finally, the call came. I was told their department was prepared to tender an offer. I asked if I could have a day to think this all over. I discussed it with my wife and we decided to accept. I had to figure out an appropriate salary to request. Not an amount they would never accept but not one much too low either. This was not easy. I called the next day, accepted the position, and requested an annual salary I thought would work. They responded the following day saying the county would agree to pay the requested amount. We determined a start date. I had done it. I met another one of my career goals. I provided my letter of resignation to an organization where I had worked for 20 years. Surprised looks on the faces of the doubters in my life were absolutely priceless. Now I had to think about so many things in anticipation of the move. There was much to consider, plan for and implement in a short span of time.

In October 2011, I left a comfortable supervisory job and transitioned to an oversight position for an entire Arizona county department. My responsibility included three large offices and one small in four different cities, along with a 45-bed juvenile detention center. Detention management was my biggest liability and continued concern. I was confident I could do the job and well, but it was a little intimidating for the first few weeks. But I overcame any fears.

There was no "how to" or operations manual waiting for me on the large desk in my new office. This turned out better than I anticipated though. I needed to make this position my own. I wanted to infuse my brand of leadership, vision, and mission into the organization. Much of what the county was doing achieved satisfactory results when I arrived. And because it is not smart to "fix" things that aren't in disrepair simply to stylize or brand things my own way, I did not. In other words, if it ain't broke, don't attempt to fix it. Instead, I turned my eye toward challenges in areas that needed adjustment or improvement. Much of it lay in my human capital – or managing people. The positive or negative impact of some staff upon their co-workers was so important to the overall success of the department.

Six years of prior experience as a unit supervisor taught

me how to effectively manage people. How to mete out progressive discipline when staff behave inappropriately. While I did not consider this an easy task, it was required at times. Most of the staff at all four offices were doing good professional work. It is the twenty percent who did not that I would need to address. The management above me did not understand the duties or headaches of a supervising probation officer. I brought this knowledge as I had worked from entry level to an administrative chief position, learning it from the bottom up. I tried to empathize with all my line officers. They appreciated that I often visited the four offices to speak with and ride with them in the field. I was a leader who cared. I always attempted to, as they say, walk the walk and talk the talk, to be a leader they could relate to and felt comfortable with. This approach had always served me well. Some leadership staff who reported directly to me were not always easy to work alongside. Others were the exact opposite. I sometimes felt I could not trust a few to be supportive of my many decisions or always have my back. Regardless, I always had the best interests of them all and the entire organization in mind. The judge who hired me brought in me in to do just that. I was never going to betray him.

With extraordinarily little public funding coming from the local county government, most of our organizational financing came from state funds. With an eight to ten-million-dollar operating budget, we didn't have enough funding to effectively operate all required department programs. However, we made it all work. We did not have a choice.

My first four years in the Chief P.O. position were a blessing. I traveled throughout the state when required, attending meetings but always making all needed decisions by email, phone, or text. It usually was 24 hours a day, 7 days a week, 365 days a year roller coaster ride, but I loved it. In year five, I sensed a judge who replaced the one who hired me wanted home-grown staff whom he knew well and trusted to oversee department operations. Not an individual like me who was brought in to improve things from outside the county. When the time was right for myself and the organization, I announced my retirement. I allowed them four months to find new leadership. This nearly five-year experience truly affirmed my beliefs about the value of having courage, patience, and perseverance.

CHAPTER 21 FURTHER READING
PERSEVERANCE

"Seek the Lord and his strength; seek his presence continually!"

- 1 Chronicles 16:11 ESV

What does continually mean? To some, it may seem like continually means when I can, when I am able, or when things are convenient for me. I know I fall prey to that notion as well. What the Lord wants from us is much more, and the results of doing what he wants are astounding.

To seek the strength and presence of God continually means that we move aside other things in favor of spending time and thoughts on him so that we can gain His wisdom, guidance, and leading. "Continually" means that there is a commitment to God's Word and living in faith by all he says, all the time. Not simply when we want to or feel up to it.

It is an unreasonable request – to always seek His presence and strength. That is the point. You will fail – but by failing God is setting you up for glory. By knowing you aren't perfect and will stumble, but continue to seek him anyway, God knows that you will turn to Him. And that is what He wants most. Your attention and love – because that is what He continually gives to you.

It is with that love and attention, that continual strength and presence that you can persevere in anything you do. And if you fail along the way? So be it. It does not and will not change His love, strength, and provision for you.

CHAPTER 22

THE OUT OF TOWNERS

Moving from a metropolitan city of one million people to a small town of 45,000 was untenable for me and my wife. Over time it became more attractive to us, but we never considered it as our permanent home. The small community was charming with appeal for residents and tourists. The historic Route 66 highway ran directly through what was once considered their downtown retail district.

Nonetheless, we bought a home and filled it with new furniture and appliances. I did this to prove my commitment to living and working in the area. We also kept our previous home five hours away. We decided not to rent it out though, as we would return to our other home a few days each month for a variety of reasons. While this was not without significant challenges, we maintained the two separate residences for almost five years. This drained much of my overall monthly income but it resulted in an excellent contingency plan.

With a demanding job, I spent a lot of time at work. My wife also worked part-time at a few places. Some things we considered weird and were often amused by was the crazy behavior of residents. The movie theater owner sometimes cancelled prior advertised movie showing dates and times on a whim. A local restaurant owner would book food chartering events and then forgot to prepare for them in such a regular manner you wondered if it was intentional. One of the dry cleaners kept unclaimed clothing for only a few days. After that it was uncertain where they went. I'd expect these business owners would not have survived if they had increased competition, but they did not. The point isn't moot from an out-of-town point of view. There seemed an attitude of this is how it is, whether liked or not. Perhaps it was rebellious inconvenience to ward off "the big city life" in some inspired way. A warning to any out of towners. Things will not go well for you here. Or perhaps it was simply oversight and nothing more.

After witnessing the "small town" ways for five years, it became apparent shops did benefit from the monopolies they created. Having lived in smaller towns and rural areas during my youth, I had seen all this before. But that was years before – and I thought at the time this crazy behavior was exclusive to those places I grew up in.

Of course, I was a different person then. Not the world traveler I had become during all my military years. It was easy to assume some of these people probably never had ventured one hundred miles from home most of their lives. But, by all accounts, they were content with their style of life. Most residents stated they wanted no commercial progress. Luddites in the metroplex world. They were happy with the way things were and the mayor and city council followed the wishes of their long-time residents. With exception of fast-food restaurants, not much in the way of retail commerce was brought to the town.

For outsiders like my wife and me, this was frustrating but there wasn't much we could do. Updated modern conveniences were certainly available in the area, but fifty or more miles away. It was a geriatric farm is what it was. Without the modernization of the rest of the world affecting commerce and industry, there was little reason for youth to stay. After high school, many younger people left seeking greater prosperity or at least, modern convenience. Who could blame them.

Ultimately, my wife and I enjoyed the odd charm of the northwestern Arizona town and we loved much about it, during our time there. My co-workers did provide me some insight and helpful tips about this high desert area. Travelling to neighboring towns made for great day trips. After arriving in October 2011, we had a unique opportunity to experience things we would not have done otherwise. We sold our home before leaving and I drove a large, loaded truck out of town the day after retiring in July 2016. We have reflected fondly on the experience. We have returned a few times to visit friends we made.

CHAPTER 22 FURTHER READING
DIVERSITY

"For just as the body is one and has many members, and all the members of the body, though many, are one body, so it is with Christ. For in one Spirit we were all baptized into one body—Jews or Greeks, slaves or free—and all were made to drink of one Spirit."

- 1 Corinthians 12:12-13 ESV

The diversity of people in this world is exciting and fills my spirit with joy. To see the different backgrounds, experiences and minds of people creates a space of love for me. While I may disagree with some positions either politically, religiously, or even morally, the breadth and width of imagination, discovery, and productivity is enough to know that there is a Creator. Going beyond that, the fact that we can all be one family, one body, working in unison for the cause of Christ makes the world even more special.

I stand in awe sometimes of the lack of love and the disdain that people can show when hurt or frightened - or even as they pursue their own selfish interests. In the same regard, I am in awe of how God can build people back up into the form that he desired when he made the heavens and the earth.

As you look at the world, imagine that each person was created individually to bring glory to God because He loved them. To varying degrees, people are successful or failures in their journey. This does not take away from the purpose of creation and how much God is jealous for their love. Remember that no matter who you encounter in the world – near or far – they have a maker. Pray for them, for their salvation, and for their walk afterward. Pray that God might restore them as he has promised you too, the believer.

PART 3: THE BEGINNING OF THE END

SAME OLD STORY

It is pointedly suggested that in the Bible most of the people talked about, whose stories are laid out for all to bare, are deplorable, selfish, unworthy, and hurt people. There is rape, torture, death, and adultery. They are flawed human caricatures whose tales we relish for one specific purpose, though seemingly via multiple layers. The Bible, in essence, seems like reading a horror story.

To read the pages is to think: "Well, at least I didn't do that." "At least I'm not in that horrible situation."

It's escapism at its root. And we feel better about ourselves for it. But the truth is there is something deeper that brings us to clarity about the people in the Bible. You see, the Bible isn't about "other people" at all; It is about you. It's about me. And it harkens back to the same old story. We are deeply flawed people who have experienced a lot in life – to what extent we learn from and use those experiences to serve others is the value of both the experiences and flaws. The people in the Bible are a tale of us.

David cheated on his wife – he was an adulterer, and then killed the woman's husband so he could marry her instead. Paul murdered people. Adam and Eve both lied directly to God. These are the people who are revered in the Biblical stories. At its fundamental core, it's only because of their path to redemption that we can follow such horrors and still hope – not because of what they did, but because of what they didn't do. What was not in their control. The Bible, then, is a story about people who don't have control, struggle to gain some, but ultimately only find it outside themselves in God.

CHAPTER 23

THE BEGINNING OF THE END

My petitions for out-of-state visitation with my daughter at age fifteen were denied. I could only continue to pay child support payments and hope the best for my first child. Indiana requires payments be made during four years of college immediately following high school. The three Indiana court hearings did provide me with an opportunity to establish more frequent contact. Although I received handwritten letters from my daughter every few months, I certainly wanted more. We agreed to have telephone conversations at least once a month. This way she could learn more about me. My ex-wife and father-in-law did extraordinarily little to facilitate these calls, so we struggled to connect as frequently as agreed. Some months we never spoke at all to one another. This frustrated me so much.

I began to question things I previously believed. It was as if half-truths and untruths filled my mind. Was she really attending college? Was my daughter getting benefit from the money I was sending? Past letters had stated that my daughter was doing well in middle and high school. The reward was her ultimately earning a full-ride college scholarship. When I began to question what was going on in her life, people encouraged me to investigate. Since she lived in a very well-controlled environment closed to outsiders it was difficult to gain information.

A phone call came one morning that validated my fears. I could hardly believe what I was being told. After graduating high school, my daughter was told she and her mother were taking a short trip out-of-state. When my daughter asked if they would return prior to the start of her freshmen year of college, she was comforted and told "yes." However, after a few weeks on the road, it became clear to my daughter this was not the case. My ex-wife had lost her mental capacity to reason correctly and was now no longer a responsible parent. While my daughter was already eighteen and a legal adult, she could have walked away. But she didn't want to disobey her mother's wishes or leave her behind and alone. It's so difficult to describe the unusual bond and loyalty that had developed over eighteen years between them. Her mother's intensity harmed my daughter in many different ways she could not imagine at the time.

I had trusted for far too long and far too much. I had believed that my daughter was being well-cared for and within "normal" homelife conditions. As normal as they could be given the circumstances, at least. I found out little of this was actually true. I felt I had been taken advantage of as much as my daughter. The enormity of betrayal was difficult for me to fully grasp. How could I have been taken for a fool for three years? My ex-father-in-law allowed it to happen. He had sent my support payments to my ex-wife, along with his own money, blurring the reality of the situation. He had funded insanity.

The beginning of the end of the craziness took place when a family member finally stepped in. A non-blood relative who cared more for my daughter's welfare than those who should have facilitated a change. My daughter told them where she was. A rescue trip was quickly launched, and my daughter was brought home. Now, the deprogramming of her mind could now begin. This would take time.

There were no kidnapping charges filed against my ex-wife. My daughter decided against it. My daughter just wanted to get away from what had happened; she just wanted to now have a normal life. Miraculously, her prior cancelled full ride college scholarship was reinstated and would begin the freshmen year she didn't get to start before. When my father and her grandfather passed in October 2008 and services took place, my daughter came to visit. We were reunited after 20 years of no unsupervised contact. The tumult and unbelievable insanity stopped and we began something different. We finally began our father and daughter relationship. This period in our lives was a long time coming. Healing for us both could begin.

CHAPTER 23 FURTHER READING
DEALING WITH PAIN

"For I consider that the sufferings of this present time are not worth comparing with the glory that is to be revealed to us." – Romans 8:18 ESV

There are few inarguable truths about life as I understand it. I will get taxed by the government, to what level of representation varies by government and my ideologies, I suppose. I will die someday – when and how I will not know until it happens, despite what late night mediums and clairvoyants suggest. I will experience joy and I will experience pain.

The last part can be the scariest and is easiest to become transfixed upon. Pain is a great motivator as I have said previously. It causes me to make inept decisions, great decisions, and everything in between. But it moves the needle, so to speak, eventually. How I go about determining how I'll most often respond to pain is up for debate. But what isn't up for argument is whether I will have it come into my life or not.

Rather than rest upon pain for the sake of pain, I choose to look beyond it to the result. There will always be consequences to life – consequences to the decisions I make. But how I get past it matters. I look to the future and God's promise. The sufferings I accumulate over my life will not be void of reason. And the end result is that it all pales in comparison to the unimaginable joy, happiness, and glory that God has for me. It may not take away the pain I feel. But the perspective allows me to move past it in ways I couldn't otherwise. With patience, some peace, and perhaps joy.

CHAPTER 24

MY THIRD CHILD: GOD'S PRECIOUS GIFT

Good resulted from a bad situation, but it wasn't always clear this would be the outcome, especially during the trials themselves. After two marriages ended in divorce, I had a beautiful daughter and son – one from each marriage. I would meet someone who became my third wife, and our marriage brought my final child into the world. I now had a wonderful son to add to his half-sister and half-brother.

However, doctors discovered early on that my son had

neurological disabilities. He struggled with infantile spasms inside his tiny brain. The prognosis: If the seizures continued, he could seize himself to death. Something needed to be done quickly. He was rushed to what was considered the best hospital in our town. After detailed examinations including several MRI brain scans, he was diagnosed with cerebral palsy. He had impairments to the entire left side of his body. We were told that our small baby boy was born with a half-functioning brain.

The condition would never improve or worsen but it would remain with him throughout his entire life. His mother and I were obviously devastated and concerned. Every parent wants their child to be perfect – or as perfect as they can be. I think healthy, happy, and secure are the ultimate goals. To have a child that was diagnosed with a disability was a frightening prospect. It changes the construct. Eventually, we just wanted our child to have a normal life, instead of perfect. It was a difficult pill to swallow – had we done something wrong? Of course not. But all manner of questions entered our minds in this situation. It felt as though the world caved in on me – as if the malady that was inflicted upon my son was my fault somehow. The mix of guilt and sadness was overwhelming at times. How could it not be? When meeting with a pediatric neurologist, we were advised of an experimental medication that wasn't approved for common use. The drug had been used to combat infantile seizure activity with favorable results, though. We consented, praying it would work.

Although the steroid-based injections rapidly increased his weight, it finally brought his infant seizures under control. After ceasing use of the medication, he lost excess weight, returning to normal size for his age. He was now out of danger and safe. These doctors had saved our baby's life. It was shared eventually that our child would have to take anti-seizure pills for his entire life. In addition to any medication, he would be custom fitted with a walking brace made for his left leg and foot. He had issues with his left hand and full vision in his left eye.

While the challenges of our son's health weren't the only issues, the burden of our child's deficiencies clearly proved too much for our marriage to overcome. We separated and eventually divorced. To characterize our marriage as having a weak bond is not fair. Nor is it appropriate. However, it was not as strong as I had expected – and shattered amid the most challenging time we'd endured as a new couple. Another loss I would now have to endure.

After this divorce, my life became almost too much for me to handle. I couldn't fathom that I'd failed at marriage for a third time. I had to find a way to move past it all. Throughout my third child's life, he's had many surgeries to improve his mobility. He's been fitted with several custom orthotics that have maximized his ability to walk. He also has met each obstacle he faced head-on with an unrelenting zest for life. He has always inspired me. Simply stated, I consider him to be a true gift from God. Other dads may have reacted differently.

I challenged myself early on to have my son's level of bravery as I meet the daily tribulations in my own life. Many in the world don't fully understand what it means to have a neurological or physical disability. Although individuals with "special needs" are treated with more respect today overall than my deaf father was when I was a child, I believe improvements can still be made. Living with a disabled father in the past, and now adult son with health challenges, has provided an undergirding to my life that has given me a perspective I don't feel I would have had without these two relationships – one that beats a drum loudly. Never quit on life and always persevere. It's a mantra that was engrained within me at a young age and reenforced and reaffirmed later in life with the birth of my third child. I've understood that life never is how we want it to be. But life has opportunities and allowed me to overcome and even succeed in ways I wouldn't have expected. Not despite the challenges of life but because of the challenges of life. As for my son? He is the beautifully perfect son after all. Just perfect in a different way than I ever could have hoped for.

CHAPTER 24 FURTHER READING
GOD'S BLESSING

"Every good gift and every perfect gift is from above, coming down from the Father of lights, with whom there is no variation or shadow due to change." – James 1:17 ESV

The amount of Love Jesus Christ has for me and for you is beyond words. What is especially intriguing to me though, is that He shares little glimpses of His love through the gifts that he provides. Often, they go unnoticed – safety, provision, caring and compassion. At other times, His gifts are glowing and radiant beams of fortune that can't be mistaken for anything other than God. Whatever the case is, no matter how great or how small, I encourage you to meditate on what he has given you and be thankful for His perfection.

CHAPTER 25

HE ALWAYS KNEW

After buying his first video camera and computer, I reminded my son he would be paying me back through equal installments, from his paychecks. My teenage son said, "I understand, Dad." From a young age, my eldest son and second of three children had figured out his chosen profession. Before leaving high school, he had a plan to get him there. He graduated top ten in his H.S. class, Magna Cum Lada, with a Media Arts college degree. Maybe the many movies his mother and I took him to as a baby influenced career choices.

At age fifteen, he started working part-time while attending school and worked a wide variety of jobs. I wanted to him to establish a strong work ethic at a young age. He really had no other choice if he wanted the expensive electronic devices that he desired. I simply did not have the financial means to provide them with my many obligations. This is the child for whom I fought for full custody as a father. The court was amenable. However, I always wanted him to have a strong and stable relationship with his mother. He needed it.

My daughter lived out-of-state and was not able, by court decision, to live or visit us. My sons and I did many outdoor activities. Playing at a park, ball games, movies, bowling, other fun activities, and time with family or friends were absolutely a part of their lives as they grew into teenagers and younger adults. I always tried to provide my children with a much different father and child relationship than I had experienced. I would later have had the same parental relationship with my daughter. I didn't know it would happen a few years later.

As a father, I cannot express the pride and respect I have

for them as adults. All three came from circumstances in their youth that could have been less stressful. Less stressful does not accurately describe the amount of trauma they each experienced as children from a divorced marital union. A reality I understood and accepted long ago is that I contributed directly to their childhood challenges. Along with the acceptance of an unfortunate reality as a child, teenager and young adult, my children had every right to a level of anger and resentment toward their parents who could not make their marriage work. It's not unreasonable to think the three children perceived us as not putting forth enough effort to make amends and reconcile.

While attending high school, my son met a beautiful, smart young lady he dated for quite some time. They eventually married. I have absolutely no doubt that they will be lifelong soulmates. Working within my son's chosen profession, required they move away and out- of-state. We visit one another, when possible. They have built a good life for themselves. But once again, my son always knew he would.

CHAPTER 25 FURTHER READING
FORETOLD

"In the beginning, was the Word, and the Word was with God, and the Word was God. He was in the beginning with God. All things were made through him, and without him was not anything made that was made." – John 1:1-3 ESV

This last chapter dealt with my son's ability to see what his future might be and manifest it to a great extent. In reality, though, my son could not take another step without God allowing him to. Nobody can. It is this power that we neglect. Only God can see the future. Only our Lord and Savior can predict what will happen to us in our successes or failure. Jesus is the only one who knows where our future lies. It is because He has always been and will always be. There is no beginning nor an end to who God is. So, take comfort in knowing that God has only good intentions for your future. He desires to bring you glory if you allow Him to. Now and in the future.

CHAPTER 26

LONELINESS

I have made many mistakes; haven't we all? I've reached out seeking support and empathy from others from time-to-time. And from time-to-time, where I thought I would find care enough to lend assistance or support, I found instead a vast barren world. Survival of the fittest. The casualties of any man's life can be brutal. The fact is, people can address matters of the heart – even overcome them, but that does not take away the event or events that happened. My past is still a part of me, whether I forgive and forget or forgive and remember. The hurt I have experienced is only a small part of the whole picture, though.

I have been labeled as an enabler (and perhaps I am), one who cannot stay away from punishment in their relationships. I have never quit on much of anything in life, just as a statement of fact. Especially when it comes to relationships. I suppose in some respects I am a glutton for a disappointment. I just do not know how else to be and have not reconciled myself to be anything different. I like who I am as a person. I make no apologies for it. Such a mindset does lead to a life of loneliness. Loneliness is sometimes good or bad.

During lonely periods of my life, I have sometimes traveled aimlessly across big cities and small towns, local, and otherwise. I've been left with images of couples "out for the evening," having a wonderful time. They are loving and respecting each other's company. I've wandered some nights like a roustabout without a compass. And very regularly, though not under my own power it seems, my car miraculously drove me home again. My safe place for me to rest.

I think this is not a tale other men have not seen. To wander and wonder – is that the plight of some men? Or are we meant to find a home that can be trusted – in our minds, in our hearts and physically. This same scenario occurs everywhere, everyday all over the world, to any number of people. A languishing search for better lives – for improvement – to not battle with the echoes of depression brought on by insecurity or disappointment with our daily life circumstances.

Life can be good. It can be great. But the rarity with which greatness is encountered is startling if I let it be. So, I don't. Instead, I focus on my family - my smart and beautiful wife, my three amazing adult children, each from past marital unions, and my frequent fellowship with my other family and friends. It is a battle every man faces. It is better when fought together. Prayers and optimism keep me going. I am a survivor and will not give up. Quitting has never been and never will be something I embrace.

CHAPTER 26 FURTHER READING
ENCOURAGEMENT

"The Lord hears his people when they call to him for help. He rescues them from all their troubles. The Lord is close to the brokenhearted; he rescues those whose spirits are crushed." – Psalm 34:17-18 ESV

Depression is a real thing. It's not something to be dismissed as we can do. How do you battle it? Through professional help, counseling and through faith. I struggle myself with doubts and challenges to my walk because of bouts of depression. Not clinically diagnosed, it is still disabling at times. The pain and darkness that encroaches takes the wind out of my sails and replaces it with leaden weight. The burdens of life take over and my mind begins to crumble at the horrors of my life, great and small.

I find solace in God's Word and His provision for encouragement. I am not alone in my grief. I am not alone in my pain. It is during those times that God is nearest to me, holding me tightest. And, while I may not feel it sometimes, I know feelings and the heart can be misleading. God's Word is true. I must live like it. And so must you.

PART FOUR: TO THERE AND BACK AGAIN

A KING'S WONKY PLAN

There was a great king who had a great kingdom. But he did not have a son, nor a wife – who had died suddenly. One day he decided he needed to find an heir to the throne. He devised a plan to find the right person. He sent for the entire population of his kingdom, and three days later, as the people gathered, said:

"Everyone will receive a pot and seeds. You must plant your seeds and the one who grows the best, more robust plant in one year's time shall have keys to my kingdom."

The king continued: "By showing me how you care for what I have given you, you will earn my respect, my trust and my throne."

The crowd cheered and went on their way.

Amongst the people, was a young boy who also received

a pot and seeds. He earnestly ran home and put soil and seeds into the pot. He watched the pot every day, watering it, fertilizing it, moving it back and forth to the sunlight.

Every day he would return to see nothing growing. Thirty days passed. Then several months. Six months, and soon it was time for the king to send word to the people again. Return with your plants and show how much value you can bring to the kingdom.

Everyone gathered in the king's courtyard again. The boy entered ashamed because he had seen so many beautiful plants. Tall ones, short bushy one. All were a vibrant green. His pot was the only one without a plant. The king entered the yard and scanned the plants. Finally, his eyes came to rest upon the boy's empty pot.

"You," the king said. "Come here."

The crowd hushed as the boy walked slowly to the front, near the king.

"What kind of plant is this? It does not grow?"

Laughter spread across the crowd. Murmurs of ridicule and judgement grew.

The king motioned for everyone to be silent. "I have found the one who shall inherit the kingdom." He motioned to the boy and put his hands on his shoulders.

"All of you were charged with taking care of what I gave you. And I see that all except one comes with a beautiful plant. However, what you didn't know was that all of the seeds had been burned and dipped in acid to ensure they were dead. They could not grow a plant. Only this boy was honest enough and had enough integrity to come back with an empty pot and dead seeds like I had given him. He chose shame over lying to his king."

The crowd was silenced in amazement.

"A man can say many things. But his heart will always be revealed in his actions. Welcome your future king."

CHAPTER 27

THE TRANSITION

When the time came, I was not necessarily prepared to handle something I had dreamed about for so many years. I was leaving the familiar, walking through an uncertain doorway, entering ... nothing.

This is how retirement felt at the beginning. No more responsibility or reporting out, no conversations with staff or tough decisions. Nothing. There was nothing there for me to hold onto. And this "nothing" is the exact reason some of my former co-workers and friends have not retired yet. They're no doubt scared. Or at least on some level, reticent to discover if they are stuck with a personal life that is lacking after their work life was so fulfilling, or busy, or…there.

My identity in who I was as an individual was linked to my work title and work world. Now that I did not have the work world to return to, the nothing I am talking about was a void that I had to learn how to fill back up. I could not imagine what those who are even more engrained in (entrenched by?) their work felt. I have known people who have said for years they will die on the job. They probably will.

In July 2016, I officially retired from paid full-time employment. My wife and I hoped earned pensions and other things we had planned financially would be enough to sustain us for the rest of our lives. As I suggested, retirement was something I thought about for years. On days when things were crazy in my work or home life, I would cajole myself forward by remembering that someday I would have a much different reality.

And now that different reality had set in.

I quickly realized how lucky I was. Many co-workers and friends just could not afford to do all this financially, in any practical manner. Retirement is not a choice. These days, a lower level of income and affordable healthcare after retiring are a primary concern. But it is only one of several financial choices, decisions and plans that can go awry. I have other friends who successfully made the transition and are doing very well. Some are hiking local mountains, traveling when they can. Some friends became photographers. Some found a hobby, a desire for doing volunteer work or have other passions.

Home projects was a major part of my retired agenda these past few years. There is a new concrete block wall behind our home now, a better organized walk-in closet with more shelving to provide more storage, the exterior painting of our home along with the sealing and painting of a covered carport were some completed projects. Time spent with my grown children is one of the best gifts that retirement has given, especially, with my disabled adult son who works full-time, lives alone, and cannot drive a vehicle. Transportation is a gift I give him at least two days a week. We really enjoy our time together.

Another treasure has been the weekly night out I spend with my daughter and son. We have grown closer and bonded more. I cannot place enough value on the precious memories we are making each week with movies, getting coffee, day trips, and meals together. One of the best ways I get time with my adult children is to travel with them. We have taken long and short trips together.

Since I now had the available time, I researched and decided to join some veterans and other service organizations with posts, chapters and lodges in my community. This includes the American Legion, Disabled American Veterans, Benevolent and Protective Order of Elks and Moose Lodges International. They all do some great work.

My wife and I have also flown, or road-tripped, to many destinations throughout the continental U.S. We travel to interesting places, take "good" photos, and share via social media as a new hobby. During my first few years of retirement, my wife and I traveled extensively. Now it is a couple of trips each year. Without the daily stressors of employment, I now concentrate on what is important – relationships, time, and love.

CHAPTER 27 FURTHER READING
IMPORTANCE OF TIME

"Humble yourselves, therefore, under the mighty hand of God so that at the proper time he may exalt you." – 1 Peter 5:6 ESV

We are all given limited amounts of time on this earth – to love, to laugh, to enjoy family, to create. I ask myself what about my use of time on a daily basis. Do I honor God with my time or do I squander it on frivolous things? I think both. But I strive to do more of the things of God with my time.

I think later in life – during retirement, in particular – time feels like it has disappeared almost entirely and mortality sets in. How many years do I have left? What will the quality of those years be? They are important questions I wish I had asked myself sooner – or, at the very least, with more fervor.

As you consider your later years (even if you are in your youth), take into consideration that reflection is the worst time to plan the future as it by the very definition is after the fact. So, be bold in the Lord. Be bold in your accomplishments. Be bold in your love for people, places, and things that God blesses you with every day and every time. It is not a void you retire to of "nothing." On the contrary, if you look at things through God's eyes, you retire to everything God has waiting for you.

CHAPTER 28

PACK YOUR BAGS

I was up-side-down and told to "kiss the stone." Considering the millions of people who must have kissed the likely disease-infested wall before me I still relentlessly swooped in for a light smack, a casual smooch of the stone below me. We were visiting the historic Blarney Castle, County Cork, Ireland, in 2004.

One of the greatest pleasures of my life has been

exploring unfamiliar places, meeting wonderful people, eating amazing food, and having fun through my travels. I have a suitcase of stickered places in my mind from all the adventures. Until I left Indiana to join the military, I had taken only a few out-of-state trips. My military years then took me to a vast network of locations. Nothing, however, compares to the trips I have taken with my wife, Erica. Over many years we have taken at least seventy-five trips, and counting. Of these, most were of the two-week-long road and hotel variety. These fortnight vacations were carefully planned events where we toured entire states. We racked up a lot of flight and driving miles, rental cars, and hotel stays. Our accumulated airline miles would give the most accomplished business traveler pause.

We saved for the travel deliberately, took photos, and enjoyed the sights and sounds. We have been asked why we traveled to some specific states. Fact is, there was always something interesting to see everywhere we went. We were simply willing to look for it.

We have toured national parks from coast-to-coast, gone to state capitol buildings, taken land, river, and sea tours, walked museums, and watched beautiful sunsets in every state we visit. On occasion, family or friends came along, but not so often. In 2010, we took a fourteen-day trip to Pennsylvania with my wife's mother and her three sisters. A wonderful experience I will never forget. It would be the last long trip my wife's aging mother ever took. A good memory for my wife and her sisters. I bonded with my mother-in-law that trip.

My wife and I's honeymoon took us to Ellis Island and the Statue of Liberty, top of the Empire State Building, a walk around Times Square and a ride on the Staten Island Ferry among other things in New York City. We have walked the Santa Monica Pier, the Hollywood Walk of Fame, drove Mulholland Drive in Los Angeles. Toured Alcatraz Island (much smaller than it appears in movies), Pier 39, and Embarcadero District, and crossed both the Golden Gate and Bay Bridges in San Francisco (much higher than they appear in movies). We have also walked along the sandy beaches in the Outer Banks in North Carolina, South Carolina, Florida, California, and Oregon. Toured many coastal lighthouses on U.S. east and west coasts. As the song by Johnny Cash clamors, "I've been everywhere, man," We always enjoy tremendous panoramic views various places provided. They made for some great pics and we were always willing to take them.

The Florida Keys and the most southern tip of the U.S., the Liberty Bell and Independence Hall in Philadelphia, PA and Mount Rushmore in South Dakota. The White Sands of New Mexico is a fascinating sight – both in view and in temperature. Alaska is a giant living postcard dedicated to the great outdoors. We viewed Mount McKinley within Denali National Park (it's the highest peak in North America at 20,310 feet) and visited some of Alaska's many glaciers. It's truly a hiking, hunting, and fishing paradise. The Grand Canyon, Painted Desert, Canyon de Chelly, the Monument Valley, and Saguaro National Monument in Arizona are spectacular. Wyoming and Montana are breathtaking, especially the Grand Teton, Yellowstone, and Glacier National Parks. The big cities, small towns, or any number of other destinations are out there to be found, if you are willing to visit them. The best quality time and shared experiences my wife and I have had are together, on the road, learning, understanding, and taking in the world. So, pack your bags, your thirst for something new, and your pocketbook. Don't be afraid of whatever adventure awaits.

CHAPTER 28 FURTHER READING
MEMORIALS

"So early in the morning Jacob took the stone that he had put under his head and set it up for a pillar and poured oil on the top of it. He called the name of that place Bethel, but the name of the city was Luz at the first. Then Jacob made a vow, saying, "If God will be with me and will keep me in this way that I go, and will give me bread to eat and clothing to wear, so that I come again to my father's house in peace, then the Lord shall be my God, and this stone, which I have set up for a pillar, shall be God's house. And of all that you give me I will give a full tenth to you."" – Genesis 28:18-22 ESV

Life is full of events and experiences that are valuable, and worthy of photos and recollection. I, along with my wife, collect refrigerator magnets from the places we visit. We have an entire spot dedicated to the memories of the places we've been. When I look at the different shapes, sizes, and colors of the various magnets, I feel happy and satisfied with what we did together, as a couple or as a family when the kids came with us. These tiny memorials are a way for us to remember the importance of what makes a difference in our lives. They are innocuous reminders that cost five dollars but are priceless. Jacob did the same thing when he thought about God. He erected a memorial as a tribute to his God. God was so valuable to his life that he always wanted to remember him in a visible, specific place. The stone represented a place in Jacob's life and should in our own. God should always take place as a significant memorial in our lives, just like our magnets or whatever it is you do to commemorate your experiences. When was the last time you made sure God was visible in your life – scripture cards, a picture hanging on the wall, or even a memento of the good God has done in your life? He is worth it.

CHAPTER 29

GIVING OF THY SELF

After my retirement home projects and other plans were complete, I began to consider what I could do next. Like most men, especially men in my stage of life, I needed projects to continue, something to pursue. Accomplishment was only an idea away. I decided to enter the world of volunteerism head on – as I would want to do in anything I attempted. As they say, if you are not first, you are some variation of last.

Although I had run into lots of challenges in my life, and at times what I would consider overwhelming odds against success, I still believed I was blessed by my Lord and personal Savior Jesus Christ. Now it was time for me to give back to individuals or organizations who needed my help as He had called me to do. Since I was a military veteran and had received VA (Veteran's Administration) healthcare over the years, I decided to help that organization first. The Tucson VA Volunteer Office offered several options on the VA campus. I put in time in different areas, but usually wound up as a concierge for information desks located all over campus. After a couple years of the VA experience, I wanted more. Needed more.

A friend asked if I would consider an unpaid position with a local private Christian school. They needed an AD (Athletic Director) for the coming school year. It involved tasks I had never done before. I accepted the challenge. I attended AD meetings and worked with conference schools to schedule boys' and girls' basketball and volleyball games. I learned to do timekeeping and scorekeeping for basketball and volleyball games. It was fast-paced and fun. I loved it. Eventually, the school year ended. I was onto my next endeavor.

Some months prior, I heard about a veteran's nonprofit organization conducting natural disaster response and recovery operations (ops) around the globe. Something else new to try. One month later, I flew to Houston, Texas for seven days to help rebuild flooded homes impacted by Hurricane Harvey. Again, it was something I had never done before. I found that if something can be taught, I wanted to learn it. Finding new experiences, learning how to do different things, and become proficient, energized my soul. Helping those in need satisfied my soul, providing a sense of purpose I hadn't felt before.

Since the relief organization's operations were based on military principles, relief efforts were familiar for veterans or easily grasped by participating non-veterans. They always provided air transport to a disaster area operation with modest provisions of housing and meals. I deployed to Houston four times and Naples and Fort Myers, Florida once to rebuild flooded homes. I was able to take a few trips when Hurricane Michael hard hit areas of coastal North Carolina, Georgia, and northern Florida. By this time, I had a few ops under my belt. In Panama City, Florida, huge pine trees snapped in half during an intense category five hurricane. This was a massive recovery op. Many lives were lost and homes destroyed or severely damaged.

I responded to a recovery op in Nebraska where an entire town was submerged under water over 30 days when a nearby river flooded. The trips were spent doing nasty, demanding work. This though, was the dirtiest, most disgusting, and challenging op I've worked. But the residents needed our help. If we didn't help them then who would?

Overall, I deployed twelve times. Since my VA and disaster relief volunteer efforts, I have worked for other volunteer organizations. These opportunities including construction and landscaping projects to improve local schools and churches. I have joined several service organizations and given of my time in support of their efforts to veterans and kids. Volunteering has taught me to be grateful, humble, and to give of myself as unselfishly as I can. The reward of volunteering is a bit of a conundrum. It makes no sense on the surface. Why spend time and money doing something that does not benefit the individual in any way – and in some cases – makes them struggle in their own life more due to expense or time spent? The answer was only clear after years of volunteering had steeped in my soul.

Interestingly, the answer is as inextricable to my own being as it was to my parents, their relationship, and my youth.

You see, my father was not the volunteering sort – he was more the "for profit of man" sort. He worked hard, tirelessly even, and left loved ones (including me) on the sidelines while he did so. But he did it out of responsibility not greed. But while his method was productive in a few ways, it was ineffective overall. This is due to my father feeling it was his "burden" to provide for his family, rather than going willingly. But that was the only way he knew how; the only way behavior was modelled to him. I have my father's drive, persistence, stubbornness, and intense focus inside me. That is clear. My makeup is hallmarked by a relentless drive to get things done, always fully completely, and without fail...even at the sacrifice of things I hold dear. To a fault, as it were, I commit to accomplishment. But I also realize I have something more cultivated than my father. More than my desire to succeed – I have a self-awareness and desire to seek Christ in a mature, in-depth way. It's not just my parents' faith. It's not because I feel I should be Christian. The thing I seek after is a path to losing myself - where I do not need to drive for results. Instead, I hope to follow Christ and He produces results for me because they are His things. And that is the answer. It always is. The volunteer work I do is simply a byproduct of my desire to follow He who called me to do work for him. So, I do.

CHAPTER 29 FURTHER READING

VOLUNTEERING

"Sell your possessions and give to the needy. Provide yourselves with moneybags that do not grow old, with a treasure in the heavens that does not fail, where no thief approaches and no moth destroys. For where your treasure is, there will your heart be also." - Luke 12:33-34 ESV

C.S. Lewis writes that we should give so much that it hurts our own economic status when he writes in his book, Mere Christianity: "I do not believe one can settle how much we ought to give. I am afraid the only safe rule is to give more than we can spare. In other words, if our expenditure on comforts, luxuries, amusements, etc., is up to the standard common among those with the same income as our own, we are probably giving away too little. If our charities do not at all pinch or hamper us, I should say they are too small." His writing echoes sentiments given in Luke, which state explicitly to get rid of everything so that you don't worship things of this world. Neither says so because they desire to hurt you personally – instead, they speak to the generosity of the heart. Do you give begrudgingly of your finances or time? That is the question I ask myself. It would be good for everyone to ask the same of themselves. It is there we can meet what we idolize more than our relationship with God. For if we cling to things of the world, we cannot cling to God as well.

Do you volunteer your time? Do you donate? Do you give to ministries and the church? Importantly, do you do so out of obligation, works, or love? I don't pose these questions to solicit guilt, but they are questions I ask myself too, as a guide to my own life.

CHAPTER 30

CLIMBING FUJI

Forty years ago, I stepped off a bus, looked at the massive pile of dirt and rocks in front of me, and took a deep breath of crisp, clean air. I was about to embark upon my climb of Mount Fujiyama in Japan. At 12,389 feet, it is Japan's highest peak. I had been stationed at Yokota Air Force Base near Tokyo for about a year. I heard the base recreation center offered tours to climb to the mountain top. I finally got time off from the military airport considered the "Gateway to the Far East." At a spry twenty-four years old, I was excited.

My now ex, but then current wife, decided not to join me on this trek. I think she feared meeting the challenge.

I was driven to the fifth climbing station of Fuji. There are ten stations from bottom to top elevation. I was advised to purchase a wood climbing stick. They were sold all over the mountain. So, I did. Before starting up the trail, I stuffed my backpack with snacks, a light jacket and first aid kit. I ensured my hiking boots were well-tied. I had read many Fuji climbers, like in our tour, began from the Kawaguchi-ko fifth station. The average climb time was five to eight hours to the summit. But I also learned the estimated time did not consider the break periods at mountain huts along the way. It by no means reflected a relaxed pace to the summit. We climbed the mountain at night with the goal of reaching the top before sunrise. There was some overhead lighting along the trail, however, most of the trail was dark, thus, my flashlight, extra batteries were needed. Doing a little research in advance of the climb and asking simple questions paid off.

As I began my ascension, I knew without a doubt I was in for a challenge. Mount Fujiyama is a dormant volcano like many mountains all over planet earth. As such, their climbing path is composed of unsteady volcanic ash and rock. As I took each step, I would slide slightly backward. This took extra energy and time. As I climbed to each station, it was tradition to have climbing sticks branded with the station number and exact elevation. It cost a few yen. The higher I climbed the colder it got, even though it was considered summertime.

At my age, I was in what I considered to be good, almost peak, physical condition. My airport job kept me busy and in shape. I was surprised as I watched Japanese teenagers running up the trail with bicycles on their backs. Later riding down the back side of Fuji. Local senior citizens climbed at a very good pace. They all were in better condition, with more stamina. I assure you it is not an easy climb. Our group of climbers did manage to reach the top before sunrise. It was exhausting, physically draining, and mentally taxing. But it was also a rejuvenation of purpose. To scale the likes of Fuji was a found sense of accomplishment that not only sounds good, *but it is good.* Like the more dangerous Mount Everest climb some undertake – it is not a task taken lightly. Not many will do the same.

Afterwards, I got some rest and drank a bottle of milk, another Japanese tradition. Then, I did it all again the following year.

It was the four-minute mile for me in many ways. Once it was accomplished, the daunting climb seemed less so. While I didn't necessarily think of the metaphor at the time, I frequently do now: climbing Fuji was how I approach life in general. Yes, there may be trepidation, concern, or worry at the base of any obstacle or event of life. There will likely be setbacks. But with careful planning, some foresight, and a lust for doing right, the world can be overcome. Not through our own power but by recognizing the Lord who strengthens our resolve, lights our path, and refreshes our spirit as we climb through life's events. I still have my beat up wooden climbing stick.

CHAPTER 30 FURTHER READING
FAITH

"Therefore I tell you, whatever you ask in prayer, believe that you have received it, and it will be yours." – Mark 11:24 ESV

What a powerful promise, encouragement, and view of faith from God. He wants to give us everything our heart desires. But because God is so gracious in His love for us, there is a caveat to protect us. We read Scripture and perhaps wonder how can this be? The answer is to read further in Scripture to understand. God provides all the answers.

You see, God desires to give us all we want but all we want is perverted until we grow in intimacy with Him. Only when we grow in our faith, mature in our thoughts, emotions, and love for the people of the world, are we able to lose the perversion and desire only goodness. It is that aligning with God's will that is the balance of the Scripture – the full rendering. God will give you all you desire because your desires are His desires. And His desires are to save the lost, to share His character of love, encouragement, and compassion. He desires to respond to those in need, to help the hopeless, and to minister to the hurt. Are these your desires? They are mine in authoring this book.

AFTERWARD

FINAL THOUGHTS ON GOD'S BLESSINGS

Throughout my life, whenever tough times came my way, I faced them head-on. Less than ideal circumstances or situations have almost always prompted my desire to overcome them in a positive way. About half the time things fell in my favor. Where did the courage, inner strength, and ability to persevere come from?

During my childhood and formative years when thoughts came to me, good or bad, I never considered their source. When good ideas benefited my life, I took in all the accolades. Things go bad? The world was out to get me. But I know I never gave up, win or lose. Regardless of the outcome, there was little gained from quitting. It was not until I became more serious in my relationship with my Lord and Savior that I began to gain an even better perspective.

It isn't even about winning or losing. Christ has already

overcome the world, and He invited me, and any who would accept Him, to come along for the victory. As years passed, my faith and trust in my Lord and Savior grew, and I understood more and more about resting in God's outcome, not mine. It became increasingly clear where thoughts in my head originated, who it was that has always been speaking to me. My abilities and successes in life, without a doubt, were all God-given. Furthermore, He wanted me to honor and praise Him with any success, rather than stop short by taking prideful credit.

In my first literary offering, I provide stories taken from life experiences. They are stories I believe worth telling and sharing with others, and do the job of honoring God for His greatness in my life, even when I didn't see it myself. Hopefully, my stories are relatable in comparison to your own life. As the title of the book suggests, I've authored stories to encourage, inspire, and help you choose to persevere in the face of darkness and understand the source of light in your life. In my opinion, there are few times in life where quitting is the correct choice. Regardless of our actions, God has never quit on us. Why should we quit on

Him?

Biblical scripture references related to each story provide understanding for how occurrences in my life and yours can provide teachable moments and an opportunity for lessons learned.

Perhaps, my stories are no different than many others. That is the point. My intent is to point to the hope you can have. I pray I've accomplished the task.

Not Afraid of the Dark

ABOUT THE AUTHOR

Darrell W. Reeves makes his initial foray into writing with a debut novel focused on perseverance, fortitude, and a desire to beat whatever challenges a scary world threw his way. Based on his own life story, this mix of memoir and anecdotal style of writing will be sure to leave you entertained, pensive and, at times, in tears. But through it all, Darrell's insight and witty approach to life leaves an indelible impression that this too shall pass. Not Afraid of the Dark is available online or at a bookstore near you.

Darrell reached a pinnacle within his profession as a Chief Probation Officer in Arizona. He had a distinguished military career in the U. S. Air Force and is currently married, and has three adult children. He resides in Tucson, Arizona where he is retired. Among Dr. Reeves's other varied interests, he now fills his days with writing, editing, and publishing.